Christianity and Political Islam

Christianity and Political Islam

MOUNIR GHABBOUR
and AHMED OSMAN

QUARTET

First published in 2010 by
Quartet Books Limited
A member of the Namara Group
27 Goodge Street, London W1T 2LD

A catalogue record for this book
is available from the British Library

ISBN 978 0 7043 7210 8

Typeset by Antony Gray
Printed and bound in Great Britain by
T J International Ltd, Padstow, Cornwall

Contents

	Introduction	1
1	The Birth of Muhammad	8
2	The Monk's Prophecy	17
3	Waraqa's Cousin	19
4	Revelation	26
5	Mecca Rejects its Prophet	31
6	Muslim Migration to Christian Abyssinia	36
7	The Deaths of Khadija and Abu Talib	41
8	Journey to Heaven	46
9	Banu an-Najjar Support their Cousin	52
10	Muhammad's Nation	58
11	The Expulsion of the Jews	63
12	Who were the Ansar?	68
13	Christians in Arabia Before Islam	77
14	Jesus in the Qur'an	81
15	Mecca Surrenders to the Prophet	89
16	The Farewell Sermon	94
17	Western Views of Muhammad	97
18	Muhammad's Islam	103
19	The Caliphate	112
20	History of the Qur'an	119
21	The Islamic Empire	123
22	Europe Hits Back	132
23	The Rise and Fall of the Ottoman Empire	135

24	People of the Book	141
25	Egypt before Islam	145
26	The Coptic Church	149
27	Egyptian Monasticism	153
28	The Arab Conquest of Egypt	158
29	Search for Identity	164
30	The Birth of Political Islam	169
31	Christians in Arab Countries	175
32	The Copts in Modern Egypt	180
	Conclusion	189
	Bibliography	191
	Index	195

Introduction

On the morning of 11 September 2001 four passenger airlines crashed in New York City, Washington DC and Pennsylvania, killing more than 3,000 people. That morning, the American Airlines Flight 11, which took off from Boston, was hijacked by five young men. At 8:45 the plane, now piloted by the Egyptian Mohammad Atta, hit the north tower of the 110 storey World Trade Centre in Lower Manhattan. On the same morning, the United Airlines plane from Boston was also hijacked by five men. This one hit the south tower of the World Trade Centre at 9:05, piloted by Waleed Alshehri from the United Arab Emirates. An hour later, with thousands of people trapped inside and rescue workers surrounding the buildings, the south tower collapsed. Half an hour later, the other disintegrated into rubble.

While this was going on, a United Airlines plane from Washington was hijacked by five men led by Hani Hanjour, another pilot from the United Arab Emirates, and hit the nerve centre of the US military at the Pentagon. A fourth plane belonging to United Airlines was hijacked by four men led by Lebanese national Ziyad al-Jarrah, but it did not reach its target and fell in Pennsylvania.

This onslaught was the bloodiest assault on the United States since the Japanese attack on Pearl Harbor in 1941. All nineteen suicide hijackers involved in the attack were young Muslim students in their twenties, except their leader Mohammad Atta who was thirty-three. Other than the four pilots who came from Egypt, Lebanon and the Unites Arab Emirates, the rest of the hijackers came from Saudi Arabia, the home of the two holy shrines of Islam. Soon it became clear that the attacks on the US, which took about two years to plan, were the work of al-Qa'ida, masterminded by Osama bin Laden its Saudi leader.

Two months later, in mid-November, a victorious bin Laden spoke of these events to a supporter somewhere in Afghanistan. Bin Laden's video-taped comments clearly confirmed his involvement:

> At the exact time of the attack on America, precisely at the time . . . We calculated in advance the number of casualties from the *enemy*, who would be killed on the position of the tower. We calculated that the floors that would be hit would be three or four floors. I was the most optimistic of them all . . . due to my experience in this field, [Osama was a construction expert] I was thinking that the fire from the gas in the plane would melt the iron structure of the building and collapse the area where the plane hit and all the floors above it only. This is all that we had hoped for . . . when the event took place. We had notification the previous Thursday that the event would take place that day. We had finished our work that day and had the radio on. It was 5:30 pm our time [in Afghanistan] . . . Immediately, we heard the news that a plane had hit the World Trade Centre. We turned the radio station to the news from Washington. The news continued and no mention of the attack until the end. At the end of the newscast, they reported that a plane just hit the World Trade Centre . . . After a little while, they announced that another plane had hit the World Trade Centre. The brothers who heard the news were overjoyed by it . . . Mohammad Atta from an Egyptian family was in charge of the group . . . All the brothers who conducted the operation knew was that they had a *martyrdom* operation: we asked each of them to go to America but they didn't know anything about the operation, not even one letter. But they were trained and we did not reveal the operation to them until they were there and just before they boarded the planes . . . Those who were trained to fly didn't know the others. One group of people did not know the other group . . . They [the brothers] were overjoyed when the first plane hit the building, so I said to them: be patient. The difference between the first and the second plane hitting the towers was twenty minutes, and the difference between the first

plane and the plane that hit the Pentagon was one hour.
(*The Times*, London, 14 December 2001)

All the terrorists who took part in the September 11 attacks came from Arab Islamic countries. When we try to understand why these young men were ready to sacrifice their own lives in order to kill people whom they didn't even know in America, we find more than one explanation. Mohammed Atta, the leader of the hijackers who supervised and carried out the attacks, clearly indicated that their aim was to establish the dominance of Islam in the world.

Osama bin Laden, who masterminded the attack, also spoke of defending Islam as being the reason behind the tragedy. In a video message released on 26 December 2001 to mark three months since the attacks on New York and Washington and two months since the beginning of the US-led military action in Afghanistan, bin Laden accused the West of loathing Islam. In the recording, broadcast by the Qatar-based satellite television station al-Jazeera, he called on his followers all over the Arab world to step up the *jihad* against the West by attacking America's economic interests, and disclosed the new thrust of his *holy war*. The leader of Al-Qa'ida praised the hijackers, whom he said 'carried out a great job', and described the September 11 attacks as 'blessed hits against international *infidelity*, and America its head'. He saw these attacks as 'a reaction against injustice [committed] against our brothers in Palestine, Iraq, Somalia, South Sudan and others such as Kashmir and Assam'. He also foretold the end of the United States in the near future. (*Asharq Al-Awsat*, London, 28 December 2001)

For bin Laden and his followers, this was a religious war, a war to defend Islam against *infidels* and against the United States, the greatest power in the world of the infidels. The religious motive was further confirmed when the American security authorities discovered three copies of a personal note left by the suicide hijackers, a copy of which was found in Mohammed Atta's suitcase left at the airport. The note included some steps to be taken by the terrorists in their preparations and rituals to be performed, including recitation of two specific *suras* (chapters) of the Qur'an.

The two *suras* comment on the wars between the Prophet Muhammad and the Unbelievers of Mecca, which took place about fourteen centuries ago. The hijackers who attacked New York believed they were fighting the *unbelievers*, enemies of Allah, in the New Mecca of the world. The *suras* included these verses:

> Fight and slay the *Pagans* wherever ye find them, and seize them, beleaguer them and lie in wait for them in every stratagem . . . Fight them, and Allah will punish them by your hands, cover them with shame, . . . Allah hath purchased of the Believers their persons and their goods; for theirs (in return) is the Garden (of Paradise): They fight in His cause, and slay and are slain: A promise binding on Him in Truth. [9:5; 14; 111]
>
> I will instill terror into the hearts of the *Unbelievers*: Smite ye above their necks and smite all their finger-tips off them . . . It is not ye who slew them; it was Allah. [8:12; 17]

Not all Muslims, however, share the hijackers' views of a holy war to defend Islam in modern times. Although there was a general cheer in the Arab world for what they regarded as the punishment of America, bin Laden's call for a mass rise against US interests fell on deaf ears. Nevertheless, the general attitude of the Arab media took a defensive position in response to the American war on terror. Arab League Secretary-General Amr Moussa denied any Muslim or Arab involvement in the September attacks: 'Nobody knows for sure who carried out these attacks, or why . . . From the very first instance, the voices of certain lobbies and quarters rushed to accuse Arabs and Muslims . . . despite there being no evidence for such allegations.' Moussa, who was repeating the same views generally expressed in the Arab media, even justified the terrorist attacks on America: 'It would be unrealistic to ignore the overwhelming frustration in the region that comes from the US administration's tendency to support Israeli policy indiscriminately.' (*Al-Ahram Weekly*, Cairo, 20 September 2001)

Osama El-Ghazali Harb, an Egyptian political commentator, also criticised the United States: 'Have the Americans learned anything from September 11? . . . It is time for the Americans to examine what happened, and to understand . . . why did it happen? Two competing answers emerged . . . One blames the pro-Israeli bias of US policy in the Middle East. The other claims that Arab and Muslim societies are naturally prone to "terror" . . . The Americans should also realise that the attacks of September 11 were closely related to half a century of US bias towards Israel.' (*Al-Ahram Weekly*, Cairo, 27 December 2001)

The call for *Jihad* (holy war) against the West in Islamic countries led Samuel P. Huntington, the Eaton Professor of the Science of Government, to conclude that world politics is entering a new phase, in which the great divisions among humankind and sources of conflict will be neither ideological nor economic, but cultural. He predicted that the clash of civilisations will dominate global politics along the cultural fault lines separating civilisations from one another.

Bernard Lewis, another leading Western scholar of Islam, has reached a similar conclusion: 'This is . . . a clash of civilisations – that perhaps irrational but surely historic reaction of an ancient rival against our Judeo-Christian heritage, our (Western) secular present, and the worldwide expansion of both.' ('The Roots of Muslim Rage', in *Atlantic Monthly*, 266, September 1990)

In *The Crisis of Islam*, Lewis writes: 'According to one school of thought, after the collapse of the Soviet Union and the Communist movement, Islam and Islamic fundamentalism have replaced them as the new major threat to the West and the Western way of life. According to another school, Muslims, including radical fundamentalists, are basically decent, peace-loving, pious people, some of whom have been driven beyond endurance by all the dreadful things that we of the West have done to them.' As the September tragedy and the continuous attacks by al-Qa'ida in different parts of the world are committed in the name of Islamic Jihad, they raise questions regarding the nature of Islam and its teaching. Committed by suicidal zealots, these attacks have served to focus world attention on Islam, one of the world's great religions, and the nature and origin of Islamic belief. Does Islam really represent a threat to the West and its modern civilisation?

Religion is commonly regarded as a person's relation to a holy God or spirit, which involves belief, worship, and moral conduct. Present day Islamic teaching, however, offers, not a spiritual but a political understanding of religion. A Saudi Arabian encyclopedia states that: 'Religion is the language of rule, government and management . . . (it) is a divine position which guides to the true beliefs and good behaviour and deeds.' (*Global Arabic Encyclopedia*, Encyclopedia Works & Distribution, Riyadh, Saudi Arabia, 1996, v. 10, p. 568) The general understanding of Islam according to the Qur'an and the life of the Prophet Muhammad makes it:

> A monotheistic religion established on belief and practice. Belief involves six principles: God, His angels, His Prophets, the Holy Scripture, the Last Day and pre-determination of good and evil. The religious duties centre upon five canonical obligations: the affirmation that there is no God but Allah and that Muhammad is His messenger; the observance of prayer; the payment of alms (Zakat); fasting the month of Ramadan and the pilgrimage to Mecca.

However, the Saudi encyclopedia talks of Islam as: 'a complete system which arranges the affairs of the individual; religious and worldly matters. It deals with his *shari'a* laws in every direction of life in the society; whether political, economic, military, social, or educational.' (*Global Arabic Encyclopedia*, v. 2, p. 45)

As we can see, while some Islamic leaders condemn these attacks as contradicting the teaching of Islam, other Muslim politicians praise it as the duty of every Muslim to kill the unbelievers. This difference of opinion shows that two forms of Islam now exist in the Middle East; a religious form and a political form.

At the same time as attacking Western Christian nations, Political Islamic groups are putting pressure on the Christian communities living in the Arab World. Although, unlike Western Christians, they have not been accused of being infidels, tens of thousands of Arab Christians from Lebanon, Iraq, the Palestinian West Bank and Egypt have had to leave their homelands, looking for safety in the West. Egyptian Copts, who represent the largest Christian minority in the Arab countries, have been put under increasing pressure both in their lives and in their worship.

In order to understand Islam, we have to examine the roots of the religion that was proclaimed by the Prophet Muhammad in Mecca over fourteen centuries ago and investigate its relation to Judaism and Christianity. Who was Muhammad, whose followers now exceed one billion in the Middle East, Africa, Europe, the Indian subcontinent, the Malay Peninsula and China? And why did he claim to be the last of the line of prophets mentioned in the Bible?

What is Islam and what is its teaching? Is it a religious faith or a political movement?

1

The Birth of Muhammad

It was Muhammad who, about fourteen centuries ago, established the religion of Islam, claiming to be the last successor of a long line of biblical prophets as well as a descendant of Abraham – the founding father of the tribes of Israel – through Ishmael, born by Hagar, the Egyptian maid of Sarah, Abraham's wife. Muhammad bin Abdullah of Banu Hashim, the founder of Islam, was born in Mecca in 570 and died in Medina in 632.

During the early years of the European Middle Ages following the fall of the Western Roman Empire in 480, Arabia Deserta ('Desert Arabia') witnessed the dawn of a new era in its long history. The Arabian Desert, a vast wilderness stretching from Yemen to the Persian Gulf and from Oman to Jordan and Iraq, occupied most of the Arabian Peninsula with an area of 2,330,000 square kilometres (900,000 square miles). Its climate was extremely dry, and temperatures varied between extreme heat and seasonal night time freezes. At the time of Muhammad's birth, most of the people of central Arabia were nomadic, but here and there were oases with settled communities and townships. Certain towns and settlements held a special importance because they lay in favoured oases or housed religious shrines, to which local tribesmen would make annual pilgrimages. Foremost among these were Mecca and Yathrib (Medina). Such places provided safe havens for trading caravans between Syria/Palestine in the north and Yemen in the south.

Mecca, where Muhammad was born to the tribe of Quraysh, lies in a barren hollow in central Arabia, between two ranges of steep hills in the west of present-day Saudi Arabia, about 1,000 miles (six weeks travel) south of Palestine. In those days, Mecca was a local pagan sanctuary of considerable antiquity. Religious rituals revolved around the Kaaba, still central in Islam today, which Muslims believe was originally built by Abraham and his son Ishmael. The Quraysh trace their origin to the progeny of Ishmael, who lived around the fifteenth century BC. According to the Book of Genesis, when she gave birth to Isaac, 'Sarah saw the son of Hagar the Egyptian, which she had given unto Abraham, mocking. Wherefore she said unto Abraham, Cast out this bondwoman and her son.' (21:9–10) Abraham then 'took bread, and a bottle of water, and gave it unto Hagar, putting it on her shoulder, and the child, and sent her away: and she departed, and wandered in the wilderness.' When the water was finished, Hagar, who expected Ishmael to die from thirst, wept and prayed to God to save her son. In this critical moment of desperation:

> . . . the angel of God called to Hagar out of heaven, and said unto her . . . fear not; for God hath heard the voice of the lad where he is. Arise, lift up the lad, and hold him in thine hand; for I will make him a great nation. And God opened her eyes, and she saw a well of water; and she went, and filled the bottle with water, and gave the lad drink. And God was with the lad; and he grew, and dwelt in the wilderness, and became an archer . . . and his mother took him a wife out of the land of Egypt. [Genesis, 21:17–21]

The Descendants of Ismael

According to Islamic traditions, the wilderness where Hagar went with her son was the area of Mecca, and the water well that appeared to her was the Well of Zamzam. When Ishmael grew up, he worked with Abraham his father to build the Kaaba sanctuary in Mecca near the well. Eventually, the area around the Zamzam and the Kaaba grew into the trading city of Mecca. Since then, Ishmael's descendants in the city, the great ancestors of Kuraysh, became guardians of the holy Kaaba, whose four corners face the four cardinal directions of the compass. It is a large masonry structure in roughly the shape of a cube, built of granite from the hills near Mecca. The holy Black Stone, possibly the remnant of a meteorite, was placed in its eastern corner. It is believed that some time later the Kaaba was used as a repository for 360 idols of Arabia's tribes, including Mecca's most important god Hubal. Once a year, tribes from all around the Arabian Peninsula converged on Mecca to perform the Hajj ritual. To keep the peace among the perpetually warring tribes of Arabia, Mecca was declared a sanctuary where no violence was allowed within twenty miles (thirty-two km) of the Kaaba. This war-free zone allowed Mecca to thrive not only as a place of pilgrimage, but also as a trading centre.

With the passing of time, Ishmael's descendants lost their role as the custodians of the sanctuary of Kaaba and for several generations, they were spread about among other tribal groupings. Before the end of the fifth century AD, however, they were able to regain their role over the holy sanctuary, thanks to Qusai bin Kilab. Qusai, who lived in Mecca from about 400 to 480 AD, became the custodian of the Kaaba after having expelled the tribes of Bani Bakr and Khuzaa out of the city. He then gathered the dispersed Ishmaelite tribes who settled in Mecca. From that point onwards, the descendants of Ishmael became known as the Quraysh. Thus Qusai became the master of Mecca and the guardian of the holy sanctuary of the Kaaba before the end of the fifth century AD. He rebuilt the Kaaba from a state of decay, and persuaded the Meccans to build their houses around it. He also established the first 'town hall' in the Arabian Peninsula, where leaders of different clans met to discuss their social, commercial, cultural and political matters. Qusai created laws so that pilgrims who came to Mecca were supplied with food and water, subsidised by a tax that he persuaded his people to pay. He had four sons: Abd Ad-Dar, Abd Al-Uzza, Abd Qusai and Abd Manaf.

As a result of these new arrangements, Mecca became a prosperous trading city in the sixth century AD, as well as the main Arabic centre of worship. Placed in a most strategic geographical position astride one of the greatest arteries of world trade, Mecca was ideally situated for long-term business ventures. It stood conveniently at the crossroads of the two major trade routes of Arabia: the Hijaz Road, which linked the Arabs with the Levant in the north, and the Najd Road, which linked them with Iraq. The prestige of the Kaaba brought many Arabs on the *hajj* (pilgrimage) to Mecca each year and the Sanctuary created a climate that was favourable to trade.

Hashim and Salma

It was Hashim bin Abd Manaf, one of Qusai's grandsons, who obtained the right to superintend the feeding and watering of the pilgrims in Mecca, thus gaining power and respect. It is said that Hashim, who was also Muhammad's great grandfather, was the first merchant to establish the practice of biannual trade journeys for Meccans; the winter journey to Yemen in the south and the summer journey to the Levant in the north. Hashim was a merchant who travelled to the Levant in the north with his caravan once a year. During one of his trips, he passed by the city of Yathrib, where he stayed for few days. Yathrib, which later became known as Medina, was a fertile oasis, slightly over two hundred miles north of Mecca, with numerous palm-trees and some cereal crops. The city was an important centre for agriculture, with intensive cultivation and clusters of oases. A large Jewish community lived in Yathrib, divided into three major clans and some minor groups.

While in Yathrib, Hashim met a noble, influential, and surely very attractive lady of the Najjar tribe, Salma daughter of Amr. Although he was already married, Hashim fell in love with Salma and wanted to marry her. At last she agreed to marry him, on condition that she would remain in control of her own affairs and live in her city. He agreed. It was this marriage between Hashim and Salma that started what became known as the Hashemite line of decent (Banu Hashim), which was to produce the Prophet of Islam and establish a blood relation between the Quraysh and the Najjar.

Hashim left Yathrib a few days after his marriage, but made frequent trips to the city to stay with his wife Salma. However, during one of his trade journeys to the Levant, Hashim was taken ill. He died in the city of Gaza, in Palestine. Salma, who was pregnant at the time, later gave birth to a son whom she named Shayba, who lived with his mother in Yathrib.

In Mecca, Hashim had a younger brother called al-Muttalib, who assumed his brother's position as the guardian of the Kaaba. Some years later, when Shayba reached the age of puberty, al-Muttalib went to Yathrib to bring his nephew to Mecca. The boy, however, refused to go with his uncle without his mother's consent. Only when she realised that her son would succeed his uncle and inherit his position as guardian of the Kaaba did Salma agree to let Shayba leave with al-Muttalib. When al-Muttalib returned from Yathrib with the young boy, the Meccans thought that he had bought a slave, and for this reason they called the boy Abd al-Muttalib. When al-Muttalib died, his nephew took over his father's position as the guardian of the holy Sanctuary and became the head of the Hashemites. Abd al-Muttalib exhibited all the qualities which had made the names of his father great and famous. It was he who, after it had been lost for hundreds of years, relocated the position of the Zamzam Well by the Kaaba and used its water. According to Arab historians, the well, except for a few periods when it dried out or was buried under sand, has been in use since the time of Abraham and his son Ishmael. Abd al-Muttalib was charged with looking after the well and the pilgrims coming to Mecca.

Banu an-Najjar, the Helpers of Abd al-Muttalib

According to Muhammad ibn Jarir al-Tabari, the tenth-century Muslim historian and exegete of the Qur'an, Nawfal, Abd al-Muttalib's paternal uncle, took possession of a courtyard belonging to his nephew, and refused to hand it back. Unable to find justice in Mecca, Abd al-Muttalib wrote to Banu an-Najjar, his maternal uncle in Yathrib, asking for help. When he received this message, Abu Sad ibn Udas an-Najjari, his maternal uncle, led eighty riders to help his nephew in Mecca:

> When Abdul Muttalib heard of this, he went to meet him and said, 'Come to my home uncle!' 'Not before I have met Nawfal,' he replied. 'I left him in the Hijr among the sheikhs of Quraysh,'

> said Abdul Muttalib. Then his uncle went and stood ne Nawfal, unsheathed his sword, and said, 'By the Lord of th edifice, either you return his courtyard to my sister's son, or my sword will drink its fill of your blood!' 'By the Lord of this edifice,' said Nawfal, 'I shall return his courtyard, and I call upon those present to witness this.'

Abdul Muttalib is said to have recited the following lines:

> Mazin, the Banu Adi and Dinar
> Banu Taym al-Lat refused to accept that I should be wronged,
> As did the lords of Malik (of Ban an-Najjar); and after this Nawfal
> Withdrew his pretension to my property
> Through them God returned my courtyard to me
> Though they were not as closely related to me as
> My own tribe.

[*The History of al-Tabari*, vol. 6, translated by
W. Montgomery Watt and M. V. McDonald,
State University of New York Press, 1988, pp. 12–13]

The woman who saw the light

Abdul Muttalib grew up to be a wise and respected man. He had five wives and ten sons, of whom three – Abu Talib, Az-Zubayer and Abdullah – were with Fatima daughter of Amr, a Quraysh sub-clan. When Abdullah was about seventeen years old, his father thought it was time for him to marry. He chose Aamina daughter of Wahb of Bani Zuhra, a Quraysh clan, to be his young son's wife. Shortly before his marriage to Aamina, however, Abdullah was offered marriage by another woman. Ibn Hisham cites the eighth-century historian Ibn Ishaq: when Abd al-Muttalib took Abdullah his son to marry Aamina, they passed a woman who was standing by the Holy Kaaba. She looked at the boy's face and said: 'Where are you going Abdullah?' When he told her, she offered him a hundred camels to marry her instead. However, Abdullah rejected the woman's offer, saying that he could not disobey his father.

ued on his way and married Aamina. When the consummated, Abdullah left his wife and went who had offered to marry him before. He was lidn't repeat her marriage offer, and asked her: ffered today what you offered me yesterday?' ...oman, no longer interested, explained that when she saw him the first time, she saw light in his face. Now, after his marriage to Aamina, the light had left him.

It is only when we know her identity that we can appreciate the importance of this story. For the woman who desired to bear Abdullah's son was the sister of Waraqa, the Christian priest of Mecca. Waraqa bin Nawfal and his sister were from the bani Asad family and were parental cousins of bani Hashim. Both clans descend from the same grandfather, Qusai the master of the Quraysh. While Abdullah belonged to the Abd Manaf's Hashemite line, which intermarried with the Banu An-Najjar of Yatherb, Waraqa and his sister were part of the Asad bin Abd al-Uzzy, many of whom converted to Christianity. Whether this story represents a historical event or not is irrelevant. What it shows is that the Prophet's early companions believed that his birth was expected. Readers of the various biographies of Muhammad will notice that after the marriage between Hashim and Salma, many prophecies expected a prophet to come from the line of Hashim. The strange thing, however, is that all of these prophecies came from one side: the Christians.

The birth of the orphan

Shortly after his marriage, Abdullah had to leave his pregnant wife to go on a trading caravan to the Levant. On his way back, he fell ill in Yathrib, where he remained with his relatives of Banu An-Najjar who took care of him. Abdullah's illness was fatal, however, and he died in Yathrib and was buried there. When she heard the news of her husband's death, Aamina, who was going through the late months of her pregnancy, became distraught and began to weep continuously. Her housemaid, Umm Ayman, nursed her through her grief but was perplexed as to what else she could do to help the young widow. About two months after the death of her husband, Aamina gave birth to a baby boy who was named Muhammad. According to Muslim historians, he was born on Monday 12th of Rabi'ul-Awwal in the year of the Elephant; this is believed to be sometime in April, 570 AD.

It seems that the child's birth was also expected in Yathrib, the city of his maternal uncles. Ibn Ishaq relates that Hassan bin Thabit, a Yathrib poet who became Muhammad's companion, said regarding the day of the Prophet's birth: 'By God, I was a well-grown boy of seven or eight, realising all that I heard, when I heard a Jew yelling out raising his voice as much as he could, from the top of a fort in Yathrib, "O Jews", until they were gathered to him, and said, "Woe to you, what has happened?" He replied, "Tonight has shined a star with which Ahmed has been born." ' (Sirat Ibn Hisham, *Biography of the Prophet*, Part 1: The Birth of the Messenger of Allah)

Upon the boy's birth, Aamina summoned her father-in-law, Abd al-Muttalib, who took the newborn to visit the Holy Kaaba for blessing. His grandfather then found a foster-mother for the baby, Halima, a Bedouin nurse from the tribe of Banu Sa'ad, who took him to live with her in the desert, and suckled him in early childhood. When he was five years old, Halima brought Muhammad to his grandfather in Mecca, who handed him to Aamina.

Once the child was returned to his mother, she was happy to be reunited with her son, and took him to visit his father's tomb in Yathrib. There she acquainted him with his extended family, his father's maternal uncles from the Banu An-Najjar, and introduced him to the city. After a one month stay in Yathreb, Aamina and her son prepared to return to Mecca. After they had travelled twenty-three miles, Aamina fell ill by the village of Abwa', where she passed away and was buried. Thus, at the age of six, Muhammad became fully orphaned. The child was left only with Umm Ayman, his mother's maid, who returned him to live with his grandfather by the Kaaba. However, Muhammad did not stay long in his new home, as Abd al-Muttalib died two years later. With no one to take care of him, he was sent to Abu Talib, his father's full brother who became the new leader of Banu Hashim. He remained in his uncle's house for seventeen years.

2

The Monk's Prophecy

Abd Manaf, Muhammad's uncle who is known as Abu Talib, assumed his father's position and became the new head of the Banu Hashim clan. Following the death of Abd al-Muttalib, Abu Talib took his young nephew under his custody, as he was only eight years old. According to Ibn Ishaq's account, as recorded in the biography of Ibn Hisham, a short time later Muhammad was taken by his uncle on trade to the Levant. There, in a Christian land we meet the first reference to the boy's future Prophet-hood, which came from a Christian monk.

One day, when the boy was either nine or twelve years old, Abu Talib decided to go out on the summer's trade journey to the Levant. When the caravan was ready for departure, Muhammad attached himself to his uncle and refused to leave him. Abu Talib therefore decided to take his nephew with him on his first trade journey. A few weeks later, the caravan reached the area of southern Syria, which had been part of the Nabatean kingdom until it was annexed by the Romans at the beginning of the second century AD. The Nabateans were Arabs whose kingdom had extended from Hijaz in the south to Jordan and southern Syria in the north. They spoke Aramaic and were converted to Christianity about two centuries before the rise of Islam.

As he had done on previous occasions Abu Talib decided to camp by a tree in this area near the city of Bosra, not far from a monk's cell. The monk, whose name was Buhayra, was known for his knowledge of Christianity, attained though the ancient books he had. Although previously when they had passed him, Buhayra never came out of his cell or took any notice of the caravan, on this occasion his reaction was completely different. Not only did he come down to meet them, he even invited them to a great feast at his cell.

The reason for this change in the monk's attitude is explained as follows: while Buhayra was watching the arrival of the caravan from his cell, he saw them approaching and noticed that young Muhammad was overshadowed by a cloud. Later, when they sat in the shadow of a tree nearby, he noticed the branches of the tree moving around until its shadow had covered the boy. When he noticed what was happening, Buhayra decided to examine the boy himself and came down from his cell to invite them all for a meal. He was disappointed, however, when they all came to him except the boy, whom they left behind sitting under the tree looking after their baggage. When Buhayra insisted that he should also come, they brought Muhammad to the feast.

Buhayra kept looking at the young boy, watching his body trying to see if he could find a sign that would identify his character. When they finished eating and dispersed, Buhayra went to the boy and asked him, swearing by al-Lat and al-Uzza, the two deities worshipped by the Quraysh, to answer his question. Young Muhammad replied: 'Don't ask me by al-Lat and al-Uzza, for by Allah I detest nothing more than these two.' Buhayra then said: 'By Allah, tell me what I ask you'; and went on asking the boy about himself and his affairs in general. It seems that Muhammad's answers agreed with what Buhayra knew of an expected prophet. When the monk looked at the boy's back, he found more confirmation, the 'Seal of Prophet-hood' lying between his shoulders.

The monk then went to Abu Talib and asked him about the relationship between him and the boy. When Abu Talib said that Muhammad was his son, Buhayra didn't believe him: 'No, he is not your son. The father of this boy should not be alive.' So Abu Talib told him that the boy was his nephew and that both his parents were dead. Now that Buhayra had found the signs he was looking for, he told Abu Talib: 'Go back with your brother's son to his country and protect him cautiously. Great things are in store for your nephew.' (Sirat Ibn Hisham, *Biography of the Prophet*: part 1, The Story of Buhayra).

3

Waraqa's Cousin

Although Waraqa's sister failed to marry Abdullah and bear his son, twenty five years later Khadija, Waraqa's cousin, was able to marry Muhammad, Abdullah's son. Khadija daughter of Khuwaylid was a rich lady and a business woman, who hired men to take her merchandise to the Levant and Yemen. At the age of forty, she had already been married and widowed twice, to Abu Hala Al-Tamimi and Atiq bin Abid al-Makhzumi, both of whom, as well as her rich father, left her a great deal of money. (Tabarani, Majma' az-Zawa'id, 2/219; al-Isti'aab, Ibn Abdul Bar, 4/219)

The family of Asad, grandfather of both Khadija and Waraqa, were not polytheists but believed in the one God of Abraham. Unlike other Meccan families, they never worshipped idols. The different accounts of Muhammad's life make it clear that they were expecting the appearance of a prophet in Arabia who would abolish the worship of idols and reintroduce Abraham's God. From the time Hashim of the Quraysh got married to Salma of Banu An-Najjar, they believed the expected prophet would come of Hashim's line. The women of Asad's family considered it a great honour that one of them should be associated in marriage with the future prophet. Although Waraqa's sister failed to marry Abdullah, Hashim and Salma's grandson, Waraqa's cousin succeeded in marrying Muhammad, Abdullah's son.

According to Ibn Abbas, the women of Mecca used to celebrate a certain feast in the month of Rajab. While they were preparing, Khadija among them, a man approached them and said: 'O Mecca's women, a prophet will appear in your country called Ahmed. Whoever of you can marry him should do so.' All the women except Khadija were upset and spoke roughly to the man. (Al-Tabqat al-Kubra, ibn Saad, 7/15)

The rich widow seemed to have desired to know Muhammad more closely. Although other than accompanying his uncle twice in his trade trips, he had no business experience, Khadija nevertheless decided to send Muhammad with her caravan to the Levant, offering him twice as much commission as she paid other agents. Muhammad, who was twenty five at the time, was happy to accept Khadija's offer. He led the trade caravan with her goods to the Levant in 595 AD. Realising that he lacked experience in concluding business deals, Khadija sent her servant Maysara with him to assist him and be his bookkeeper.

Muhammad followed the same trade route to the Levant that he had previously followed with his uncle, passing through Wadi al-Qura, Midian, and Diyar Thamud. At last, after about two months of travel, he reached the city of Basra where he had met the monk Buhayra. This time, according to Ibn Hisham, he rested under a tree on the outskirts of Basra by the cell of Nestor the monk. The monk looked at Maysara and asked: 'Who is the man beneath this tree?' 'A man of the Quraysh, from the people who have guardianship of the Sanctuary', answered Maysara. 'No one has ever stayed under this tree other than a prophet', said the monk. Muhammad stayed in Basra for about a couple of months, dealing with Christians and Jews who were trading in the city.

Although Muhammad proved to be a successful trader who made her a great deal of profit, Khadija's interest in him had nothing to do with financial matters. Muhammad's boss wanted to marry him. The reason for her desire to marry the young man is said to have been related to what Maysara had seen of prophetical signs and what she had heard of Buhayra's remarks. Khadija was a rich, attractive and firm woman, and many men of the Quraysh had tried to marry her, yet she had no intention of marrying a third time. The middle-aged widow, who refused offers of marriage from many prominent Arab businessmen, wanted to marry only Muhammad. Not expecting the young man to approach her, Khadija initiated the marriage proposal herself. She sought the advice of her friend Nufaysa daughter of Munya, who offered to approach him on her behalf and, if possible, arrange a marriage between them.

Nufaysa went to Muhammad and asked him why he had not married yet. 'I have no means to marry', he answered. 'But if you were given the means, and if you were bidden to an alliance where there is beauty and wealth and nobility and abundance, would you not then consent?' asked Nufaysa. 'Who is she?' Muhammad excitedly inquired. 'Khadija', said Nufaysa. 'And how could such a marriage be mine?' he asked. 'Leave that to me', she replied. 'For my part, I am willing', said the young man. When Khadija heard of his positive reaction, she sent him a message, asking him to come and see her. When he came, she offered herself to him in marriage, and they both agreed that he should speak to his uncles and she would speak to her uncle Amr bin Asad, as her father had died.

Muhammad was very pleased with Khadija's offer and went to tell his uncles, who all agreed on the marriage and chose Hamza (although he was the youngest, being only twenty-seven at the time) to represent them on this occasion. Hamza was most closely related to the clan of Asad, as his sister Safiyya had just married Khadija's brother Awwam. On the other hand, Khadija's uncle, Amr bin Asad, did not hesitate to make his acceptance clear. The marriage was then concluded at a dowry of twenty young camels, and a big wedding celebration followed, with a number of sheep and camels slaughtered to feed the guests.

Khadija was a middle-aged upper-middle class lady of forty, twice widowed, but she was also an exceptionally charming and a beautiful woman; as well as being rich, she was famous for her personality and good character. She was also a kind woman who fed and clothed the poor, assisted her relatives financially, and even provided for the marriage of those of her kin who would not otherwise have had the means to marry. Like many of the Asad family, she believed in one supreme deity and didn't worship idols.

Muhammad, on the other hand, was a young man of twenty five, of average height, medium stature and a fair complexion. He was of sturdy build with broad shoulders, long muscular limbs and a large head. His wide eyes were black and his eyelashes were long and thick, with exceptionally long lashes and extensive brows, slightly arched but not joined. He had a prominent forehead and thick hair with some waves that came down to his shoulders. His nose was aquiline and his mouth was somewhat large, with a thick black beard and moustache. Muhammad walked very fast, leaning forward, as if he was walking downhill. He was a lonely man who always kept his feelings under firm control, who was especially fond of children and used to get into the spirit of childish games in their company.

Evidently, Khadija fell in love with Muhammad; after all it was she who had asked him for marriage. As for Muhammad, he certainly loved Khadija dearly, so much so that more than twenty-five years later, even after her death, Ayesha, his young and attractive wife, still felt jealous of his love to Khadija. Ayesha daughter of Abu Bakr is reported to have said: 'I have never felt so much jealousy towards anybody as I did towards Khadija, even though I did not live with her.' One day, Ayesha asked him: 'Am I not better than Khadija? She was a widow, old, and had lost her looks; you love me better than you loved her?' 'No, by God!' answered Muhammad, 'she believed in me when nobody else did, she helped me and comforted me when there was none to lend me a helping hand.'

Nevertheless, it is clear that bodily desire was not the only motive for this marriage. While he needed a mother figure that loved him, helped and protected him, she believed him to be the future saviour of Arabia. Khadija and her family not only rejected Meccan religious beliefs and worship, they were expecting a new prophet to appear in Arabia, who would come from Hashim's descendants, through the line of Abdullah. That is why Khadija, following her cousin's example, offered to marry Abdullah's son. This motherly relationship becomes clearer when we know how Muhammad himself saw Khadija's relation to him. As the saying goes '*behind every great man is a great woman*'; he seems to have identified a great mother behind every messenger. According to Ibn Abbas, Muhammad said: 'The most excellent women of Paradise are:

Khadija the daughter of Khuwaylid, Fatimah the daughter of Muhammad, Asiya the wife of Pharaoh, and Mary the daughter of Imran.' [Musnad Ahmed bin Hanbal, Volume 1, page 293, Hadith 2668] As Pharaoh's wife saved and brought up Moses and Mary gave birth to Jesus Christ, so Khadija sponsored Muhammad and looked after him and Fatima brought up her two sons Hasan and Hussein.

After marriage, Muhammad left his uncle's house by the Sanctuary, and moved to his wife's house which stood at the smiths' market in an alley branching out of the bazaar behind Zamzam Well. The marriage was a very happy one, and they lived in mutual love, understanding and compassion for twenty years. By now, Khadija had become quite a wealthy lady and felt no need to keep trading and increasing her wealth; instead, she decided to retire and enjoy a comfortable life with her husband.

Five years later, Abu Talib had a new son with his wife Fatima, who delivered the baby beside the Sanctuary. According to tradition, Muhammad was the first person to see the child when he was three days old, and he named him Ali. When the boy was five or six years old, a famine occurred in Mecca, affecting Abu Talib's economic situation. It was then that Muhammad and Khadija decided to adopt Ali, who went to live with them. From that moment on, Ali did not leave the company of Muhammad, who brought him up like a son until he died.

After marriage, Muhammad had no need to travel for trade neither did he do any other job. From then onwards he was supported by his rich wife. Being a lonely man since his childhood, Muhammad had little contact with other people in Mecca and kept close to his family. Alone with no financial worries, Muhammad started to think of the world around him, and try to find answers for the eternal questions man had to face since the dawn of human life; who are we, what comes after death and who created our world? During his childhood near the Sanctuary, he had noticed that different Arab tribes came every year to visit the image of their deity, and perform their holy rituals. However, after he started to travel to the Levant and, especially since his marriage to Khadija whose family were Christians, he started to wonder which belief he should follow.

Muhammad was given to solitude and meditation on the barren rocky hills outside Mecca. Like a hermit who lives in isolation trying to reach the heavenly divine power through delving deep into his inner self, Muhammad spent much of his time on meditation. He used to wander alone in the hilly areas around Mecca, until he found a small cave known as Hira at the peak of Jabal An-Nur (the Mountain of Light), about two miles to the east of Mecca. There he would retire for days at a time, and there he spent the whole month of Ramadan every year, engaged in some form of religious devotion, with little food and water.

By retiring to meditate in seclusion on the mountain, Muhammad was following the same practice of a group who lived in Arabia during this time, who were known as 'Hanifs'. According to the early Muslim tradition, before the time of Muhammad's public appearance as a prophet, there were in Arabia – not only in Mecca and Medina but also in a few other cities – certain seekers after the truth who rejected Arabian idolatry. The word Hanif denoted the people who, although they believed in the monotheistic God of Moses and the resurrection of Christ, were neither Christians nor Jews. Wellhausen, the well known German biblical scholar, believed that the word originally meant a Christian ascetic. However, a verse from the seventh century AD indicates that Hanif is distinguished from the Christian priest and the Jewish rabbi. (Yakut, ii. 51; Kitab al-Aghani, xvi. 45)

The Hanifs, who do not appear to have been organised in a sect or community, existed in Arabia a long time before Muhammad. They did not worship idols and were known for their practice of purification by running water (ablution), like the Essenes of Palestine. Later, the Hanif appear twelve times in the Qur'an, indicating those who possess the real and true faith. The Islamic holy book uses the term *hanif* to designate the primordial monotheistic religion, the faith of Abraham as the representative of the pure worship of God, in contrast with the idolaters. In various traditions Muhammad describes the religion proclaimed by him as

al-hanifiya al-samha (mild or liberal Hanifism), in o
ascetic movements. According to Islamic belief, the Hani
spent time away from the polytheist environment and ma
retreats to nearby hills to pray, one of which was the Mour
Light where Muhammad's Hira Cave was situated.

Before adopting Christianity, Waraqa bin Nawfal, Khadija's cousin, had been a Hanif. The story starts when, at a sacrificial feast held by the Quraysh for one of their idols, four men of the tribe refused to take part in the feast and walked out. They agreed to keep their counsel in bonds of friendship. They were of the opinion that their people had corrupted the religion of their father Abraham. The four decided to stand together and go out seeking the true Hanifitic religion, the faith of Abraham. Two of the four, Waraqa bin Nawfal and Uthman ibn al-Huwairith, came from Khadija's family, the Bani Asad. They later converted to Christianity. As for the other two, while one of them remained a Hanif until he died, the other immigrated to Abyssinia where he also converted to Christianity. (Alfred Guillaume, *The Life of Muhammad: A translation of Ibn Ishaq's Sirat Rasul Allah*, Oxford University Press, USA, 1979, p. 99)

4

Revelation

A turning point in the life of Muhammad took place during the fasting month of Ramadan in AD 610, when he had an encounter with the angel Gabriel. Gabriel was mentioned for the first time in the Old Testament Book of Daniel, when he appeared to the prophet Daniel, in the shape of a man to make him understand the meaning of a vision he had had. Gabriel's stature in the Qur'an is similar to that of the angel Michael in the Bible, who is described in rabbinic literature as having been the guardian of Abraham and Moses. It was Gabriel, too, who, in the Gospel of Luke, appeared to Mary and foretold the birth of Jesus.

One night towards the end of the month of Ramadan, Gabriel came to Muhammad while he was asleep in the cave of Hira. The angel was holding a piece of cloth in his hand, on which there was some writing, and asked him to read. Muhammad explained that he was unable to read or write. Gabriel pressed him so strongly with the cloth that he was nearly suffocated, then released him and repeated his demand for Muhammad to read. Twice Muhammad gave the same answer and twice he received the same harsh treatment from the angel. Finally he asked Gabriel what it was that he wanted him to read, to which the angel replied: 'Read in the name of thy Lord who created, created man from clots of blood. Read: for thy Lord is the most beneficent, who hath taught the use of the pen, taught man what he knew not.' (96:1–5).

When Muhammad repeated what the angel said, which turned out to be the first delivered part of the Qur'an, Gabriel left. Muhammad then awoke from sleep remembering every word he said, as if it had been written in his heart.

Muhammad went out of the cave, and moved about on the

mountain. As he was moving he heard a voice calling him: 'O Muhammad, you are Allah's Apostle, and I am Gabriel.' He looked up towards the sky and saw the angel in the form of a man with crossed legs, standing at the horizon of heaven. Muhammad, not realising what was going on, froze in his position, moving neither forwards nor backwards. Trying to avoid the angel, he turned his face away. But this did not help; whichever direction he looked in, he found the angel standing there. Muhammad must have been frozen in his position for some time, for Khadija's messengers had come looking for him and left, while he was still standing in the same place. At last the angel left him and Muhammad went home. (*The Prophet's Biography*, Ibn Hisham, Part 1, p. 173)

This was Muhammad's first encounter with the angel Gabriel, when he was forty years old, and it left him unsure of exactly what he had been through. He hurried home, and sat by his wife. It was clear to Khadija that Muhammad was distressed; his heart was beating rapidly. He was uncertain as to how he should take the revelation. Khadija, who was getting worried about him, asked Muhammad where he had been. He told her exactly what has happened to him on the mount. As if realising the importance of this encounter with the angel, Khaduja didn't waste any time. While trying to reassure him, she put on her clothes and then took him out to see her old Christian cousin Waraqa bin Nawfal, who had the knowledge of the Scripture. After she explained what had happened to her husband, Waraqa asked him: 'What did you see?' When Muhammad described it, Waraqa recognised the signs of prophet-hood and told him that the angel he had seen, Gabriel, was the same one God had sent to Moses with the Law. (*Sahih al-Bukhari*, Narrated by Ayesha, Volume 4, Book 55, Number 605)

Waraqa told Khadija: 'If you are telling me the truth, he has received the Law, and he is the prophet of this nation.' He then told Muhammad: 'I wish I were young and could live up to the time when your people would turn you out.' Muhammad asked: 'Will they drive me out?' and Waraqa said: 'Anyone who has come with something similar to what you have brought has been treated with hostility; and if I remain alive till the day when you are turned out, then I will support you strongly. (Ibid., Volume 1, Book 1, Number 3)

Following this explanation, Muhammad went out to the Sanctuary as was his habit, and Waraqa followed him. They met there while Muhammad was circumambulating the Kaaba. There on the holy ground, Waraqa assured Muhammad again that he was the Prophet of Arabia, then bent his head towards him and blessed him with a kiss on the crown of his head. Thus Waraqa the Christian was the first of all people to bless Muhammad and confirm his prophethood.

Khadija, who was fifty five at the time, became the first person to believe that her husband was a prophet, even before he was called. In fact, looking at the story of their life together, she expected this development and had been waiting for his encounter with the angel since their marriage fifteen years earlier. The second one to believe in Muhammad was Ali his cousin, who was ten years old at the time, and who had been brought up by Muhammad and his wife. Ali asked Muhammad how he could become a Muslim. 'Bear witness that there is no god but Allah alone without associate, and disavow al-Lat and al-Uzza, and renounce rivals', said Muhammad. Ali did so and became a Muslim. The three of them used to go out to the Sanctuary and pray to Allah, ignoring the images of the many deities worshipped there. It is reported that one day, as the sun started rising, Muhammad was seen facing the Kaaba and started to perform his prayers. Soon he was joined by Khadija who stood behind him and Ali who stood on his right. When he bowed down, they bowed and when he stood up straight, they did likewise. When he prostrated, they, too, prostrated. (This incident is included in the books of both Imam Ahmad and al-Tirmidhi, each detailing it in his own Sahih.) It was Gabriel who taught Muhammad how to pray while he was retired on the hills of Mecca. First the angel performed the purifying ritual of ablution, and told him to do the same. Gabriel then said the prayer and Muhammad imitated him.

Following this great event in his life, Muhammad had no more visions for three years, which made him distressed. However,

Khadija his wife never lost faith in him, and see
prophetic future. It seems that those chosen
mission must undergo a three-year period of
they receive the call. St Paul, the apostle who spr
the Gentiles in the Roman Empire, had a simil
was a Jew who lived in Palestine during the fir
century AD and persecuted the followers of Christ. One day, while he was on his way to Damascus, Paul had an unexpected encounter with the risen Christ, who rebuked him for his persecution. This was a turning point in Paul's life, as he accepted Christianity and devoted the rest of his life to spreading the Christian Gospel among the nations. After having been baptised a Christian, he retired to the desert of Arabia for three years of prayer and solitude before returning to Damascus. Three years was also the time for initiation into the early communities of the Gnostic Christians in Egypt and the Levant. Those who reach the highest degree are only those chosen by the spiritual powers through revelation, and only those who receive a vision with the spirit are regarded as having reached the highest degree.

Three years after the first vision, while still meditating in the wilderness, Muhammad received his call. Gabriel visited him again, this time asking him to go out and proclaim the message of Islam publicly. Muhammad received this demand included in another chapter of the Qur'an, telling him: 'O thou wrapped up, arise and deliver thy warning!' (74:1–2) However, this time also Muhammad didn't realise quite what was going on. He hurried home to Khadijia, to tell her of the new experience:

> his neck muscles [were] twitching with terror till he entered upon Khadija and said, 'Cover me! Cover me!' They covered him till his fear was over and then he said, 'O Khadija, what is wrong with me?' Then he told her everything that had happened and said, 'I fear that something may happen to me'. Khadija said, 'Never! But have the glad tidings, for by Allah, Allah will never disgrace you as you keep good reactions with your kith and kin, speak the truth, help the poor and the destitute, serve

ur guest generously and assist the deserving, calamity-afflicted ones.'

[*Sahih Bukhari*, narrated by Ayesha, Volume 9, Book 87, Number 111]

Ibn Ishaq, the biographer of the Prophet, says that when there was resumption of Divine revelation after its cessation following the first revelation, Khadija received a Divine tribute and a salutation of peace from God. The message was communicated to Muhammad by Gabriel, and when he conveyed it to Khadija, she said: 'God is Peace (as-Salam), and from Him is all Peace, and may peace be on Gabriel.'

5

Mecca Rejects its Prophet

Three years had passed since Muhammad's first encounter with the angel, during which time he had gained only three followers; Khadija his wife, Ali his cousin and Zayd his freed slave. Then he had another visit with the angel, this time with a command from God to 'arise and warn', whereupon he began to preach in public for the first time. In AD 613, now a Messenger, Muhammad started going to the Sanctuary, where he preached his new religion; Islam. The Messenger attacked polytheism and insisted that 'there is no God but Allah', who is one and unique. It was Allah who created the world and it is He who will resurrect the dead on the Last Day, for judgment. Muhammad also asked the Arabs to be generous and help the poor in their midst. However, the Prophet gained but few members of his own family and intimate friends, and was rejected by all Meccan tribes. Muhammad's attempt to persuade his people of the Quraysh to abandon worshipping idols for the sake of his religion was a complete failure. Neither was he able to convert any of the Arabian tribes who visited Mecca every year during pilgrimage.

Allah was not a new God for the Arabs, as they had acknowledged this divinity, being one of the Arabian deities, regarded as 'the Lord of the Kaaba', to whom the Meccan Sanctuary was dedicated. In a literary sense the word 'Al-lah' (al-Ilah) means 'the god' the plural of which is 'Elohim' of the Old Testament. Even the Arabic-speaking Jews and Christians used 'Allah' as the name of God, while the Christian Arabs occasionally participated in the cult which was celebrated in the Kaaba.

Muhammad's new religion, Islam, like any other religion, was built on two main elements, belief and worship. Islam requires the belief in the unity of God who had no image, and in the resurrection of the dead on the Day of Judgment, while worship included the observance of prayer, the payment of alms (Zakat), the pilgrimage to Mecca, and fasting the month of Ramadan.

However, during the early days in Mecca, the daily prayers, which consisted of reading the scriptures, bowing, kneeling, and prostration, were offered only twice, at daybreak and sunset. Later they became five, adding noon, afternoon and night prayers. As for the Fast of Ramadan, it was introduced in Medina, eleven years after Muhammad's call. The manner of fasting was abstinence during the day, with permission to partake of food and drink after sunset. At the same time, Zakat originally meant alms giving, and the practice was unregulated. Later, in Medina, it became a prescribed obligation for the support of the poor of the community. Pilgrimage to Mecca, which had been a pre-Islamic custom, was only adopted later by Muhammad as an important Muslim ritual.

Muhammad's Followers

After the conversion of Khadijah, Ali and Zayd, Abu Bakr, who had been an intimate friend of Muhammad, was the first convert to Islam. Abu Bakr, who lived in the same aristocratic locality of Mecca as Khadija and Muhammad, was a thin man with fair skin, who had been born to a rich family two years after Muhammad's birth and became a successful cloth merchant. His conversion brought some of his friends and relatives to Islam, among whom was Uthman bin Affan, who became the third Caliph. His acceptance of Islam also encouraged some slaves to embrace the new religion, of whom he purchased eight slaves, four men and four women, and set them free.

When Muhammad openly espoused Islam, his people didn't believe anything he said. They regarded his words as fantasies and old fables. Their first reaction was to accuse him of sorcery, soothsaying, madness, and of being a poet like others who were known among the people of Arabia at the time. Nevertheless, they decided to prevent his access to those whom they feared might listen to him and follow him. When he began to speak against their gods, the Meccan authorities became actively hostile, mocking and insulting him. They incited those who called him a liar and accused him of being possessed. The Quraysh completely rejected Muhammad's monotheistic views, and responded to the message of the resurrection and the last judgment with denial and scorn: 'It is nonsense that we shall come to life again after we have become decayed bones.'

As much as they desired to get rid of him, the Meccans were not able to touch him, as he was protected by his uncle Abu Talib and his Hashemite clan, so the persecution of Muhammad personally was of a very underhanded nature. At the same time, his wife Khadija stood by him and supported him against any symptom of weakness or despondency generated by the harm his enemies had inflicted on him. His opponents had to content themselves with plotting against him in secret meetings, and with maligning and ridiculing him.

Pressure on Abu Talib

When all their efforts to persuade Muhammad to stop insulting their gods had failed, the Meccans tried to put pressure on his uncle Abu Talib to control his nephew:

> When the Quraysh saw that he would not give them any satisfaction, they objected to his departing from their ways and denouncing their gods, and seeing that Abu Talib protected him, shielded him from harm, and would not hand him over to them, a number of the nobles . . . went to Abu Talib and said, 'Abu Talib, your nephew has reviled our gods, denounced our religion, derided our traditional values and told us that our forefathers were misguided. Either curb his attacks on us or give us a free hand to deal with him, for you are just as opposed to him as we are, and we will deal with him for you.' Abu Talib gave them a mild answer and declined courteously, and they left him. The Messenger of God continued as before, proclaiming the faith of God and summoning people to it. The only consideration which prevented them from killing him straight away was fear of the blood-vengeance of the clan to which his family belonged.

After this event, Muhammad was estranged from the Quraysh,

and they withdrew from him and harboured a secret hatred for him . . . Eventually they went to Abu Talib once again. 'Abu Talib,' they said, 'we hold you in respect among us on account of your age, your nobility and your standing. We asked you to forbid your nephew to attack us, but you did not do so. By God, we can no longer endure this vilification of our forefathers, this derision of our traditional values and this abuse of our gods. Either you restrain him or we shall fight both of you over this until one side or the other is destroyed,' or words to that effect. Then they left. This breach and enmity with his tribe weighed heavily on Abu Talib, but he could not reconcile himself to surrendering the Messenger of God to them or deserting him . . .

Abu Talib sent for the Messenger of God to attend his meeting with the Quraysh. When he came in he said, 'Nephew, here are the shaykhs and nobles of your tribe. They have asked for justice against you, that you should desist from reviling their gods and they will leave you to your god.' 'Uncle,' he said, 'shall I not summon them to something which is better for them than their gods?' 'What do you summon them to?' he asked. He replied, 'I summon them to utter a saying through which [all] the Arabs will submit to them.' Abu Jahl said from among the gathering, 'What is it, by your father? We would give you it and ten like it.' He answered, 'That you should say, 'There is no deity but God.' They took fright at that and said, 'Ask for anything rather than that!' However Muhammad insisted on carrying on with his call.

'If you were to bring me the sun and put it into my hand, I would not ask you for anything other than this.'

They rose up to leave in anger and said, 'By God, we shall revile you and your god who commands you to do this!' The chiefs among them hurried about, exhorting; 'Go and be staunch to your gods! This is a thing designed . . . to the words 'naught but an invention.'

(*The History of al-Tabari: Muhammad at Mecca*,
translated and annotated by W. Montgomery Watt and
M. V. McDonald. State University of New York Press, Albany
1988, Volume VI, pp. 93–5)

Persecution

Mecca then decided to punish all those who had converted to Islam. The companions of the Prophet were hurt, while the city of Mecca became dangerous for them, their lives there unbearable hell. Many of the clans began to persecute his followers, even going so far as to boycott them. Matters were serious for those converts who were socially weak and unprivileged. 'The Quraysh showed their enmity to those who followed the Apostle. Every clan which contained Muslims attacked them, imprisoning them, beating them, allowing them no food or drink, and exposing them to the burning heat of Mecca, so as to seduce them from their religion. Some gave way under pressure of persecution, and others resisted.' (Alfred Guillaume, *The Life of Muhammad*, p. 143) One of the Meccans threw his Abyssinian slave, Bilal, onto the hot sand under the burning sun, laid a heavy stone on his chest and left him there to die, for no reason except his insistence upon his new faith. Bearing himself gallantly under this torture, Bilal kept on repeating, 'God is one, God is one.' When Abu Bakr saw him, he bought him from his master and set him free.

In the face of this unbearable persecution, Muslims started to look for a secure refuge to escape the suffering and oppression caused by polytheists.

6

Muslim Migration to Christian Abyssinia

Five years after the start of Muhammad's mission, while his followers were suffering continuous daily oppression in Mecca, it became clear that this unbearable situation could not go on for ever. Although the Prophet himself was protected by his uncle Abu Talib, he was unable to protect those who followed him or prevent harm coming to them. During this period in AD 615, while Muslims were suffering Mecca's oppression, Muhammad received the Sura of Kahf (The Cave). It told the story of some young men who, in order to save themselves and their faith from the injustice of their king, left town and went to live in a cave, looking for their safety. The believers found in this story guidance to the road they should follow to get to a safe place, away from those who persecute them in Mecca.

Accordingly, the Prophet ordered those who were vulnerable among his followers, who were the majority, to leave Mecca and migrate to Abyssinia (Ethiopia), away from the Quraysh and the harassment they were facing. Looking for a safe place to protect them, he chose a Christian country, away from the polytheists, to be assured of the protection of the Muslims and to be sure that no harm would come to them, neither in their faith nor in their life. One day Muhammad told them: 'If you go to the land of Abyssinia, it is a land of truthfulness, and there is a king no one is oppressed with him. So that God relieves you of (the suffering) you are in.' (Ibn Hisham, *The Prophet's Biography*, Part 1, p. 222)

Abyssinia was a Christian country in eastern Africa to the west of

Yemen, separated from Arabia by the Red Sea. Now called Ethiopia, its capital is Addis Ababa. In those days, Abyssinia was an extensive land with various natural divisions, which included the Eritrean coast on the Red Sea as well as Somalia and part of the Sudan. Christianity had been brought to Abyssinia by two Phoenician brothers three centuries earlier, during the rule of King Ezana. In the fourth century, Frumentius, a Christian from the Phoenician city of Tyre, in south Lebanon, was shipwrecked with his brother Aedesius off the Abyssinian coast, and they were washed ashore and taken to the royal palace. Eventually they became King Ella Amida's private secretary and royal cup bearer respectively. They served the king well, and Frumentius became regent for the infant prince Ezana when Ella Amida died. Frumentius and Aedesius were able to proselytise their Christian religion in Abyssinia and the young King Ezana was baptised a Christian. After some time, the two brothers travelled down the Nile through Egypt to the Mediterranean. While in Egypt, Frumentius contacted Pope Athanasius of Alexandria and asked him to send missionaries to Abyssinia, since the people there had proved ready to receive the gospel.

The Pope of Alexandria agreed and appointed Frumentius himself to the task, as it required someone fluent in the language and acquainted with Abyssinian customs. He ordained Frumentius to be the first *abuna* (bishop) of the Ethiopian Orthodox Church, and he became known as the *Abuna Salama* (bishop of peace). His mission was successful and with the support of King Ezana, Ethiopia became a Christian nation. Thereafter, the Ethiopian Church remained part of the Coptic Orthodox Church, and the Coptic Patriarch of Alexandria sent to Ethiopia everyone of its succeeding Abunas. This situation went on until 1959, when Cyril II, Pope of Alexandria and Patriarch of All Africa, granted the Ethiopian Church the right to appoint their own Patriarch. In other words, the Ethiopian church was ruled by Egyptians for sixteen centuries.

The first Muslim group to immigrate to Abyssinia consisted of twelve men and four women; among them was Uthman bin Affan and his wife Ruqayyah, daughter of the Prophet. They sneaked out of Mecca under the cover of darkness, so that the Quraysh would not notice them. When they arrived at the port of Jeddah, they found two trade ships which took them across the Red Sea to Abyssinia. Soon the Quraysh knew of their departure and went after them. However, when the Meccans arrived at Jeddah's shore, the Muslims had already departed on their way to Abyssinia.

This first migration of the Meccan converts proved to be successful, for they were able to keep themselves and their faith away from Quraysh persecution. This situation, however, did not last long, as the immigrants hurried back to Mecca a few months later, when they heard that the Quraysh had made peace with Muhammad. Nevertheless, when they came a few miles away from Mecca, they found this to be false news. It was just a rumour. The reason for this rumour was that Muhammad went to the sanctuary of the Kaaba during Ramadan, at a time when there was a large Meccan crowd there. While talking to them, he started to recite Surat An-Najm (The Star), and when he came to the words 'fall ye down in prostration to Allah, and adore (Him)' (the Qur'an, Verse 62), he prostrated himself, so the polytheists could not help it, and they also prostrated behind him. When the news reached the immigrants in Abyssinia, it was in a completely different form. They were told that the Quraysh had converted to Islam, so they returned to Mecca hoping to be united with their people and their folk. When they knew the facts, some of them returned (to Abyssinia) while others entered Mecca in disguise or accompanied by one of the polytheists. The Meccan authorities increased their torture of those who came back from Abyssinia, as well as the rest of the Muslims, and the Prophet advised his companions to immigrate to Abyssinia for the second time. In this second migration in AD 615, eighty-three men and ten women left Mecca. They represented the great majority of Muhammad's followers, who numbered no more than about one hundred at the time. About two dozen Muslims remained in Mecca, including Abu Bakr and Ali as well as the Prophet and the members of his family.

The Meccans did not give up, but tried to get back Muhammad's followers who had reached Abyssinia. They sent two men, Amr ibn al-As and Abdullah ibn Abi Rabi'a, to Negus (the king of Abyssinia) to try and get them back. The two delegates carried with them many expensive gifts for the priests of the church, and were advised not to meet Negus until they had given those presents to the bishops and convinced them of their viewpoint, so that they would support them before the king. When they had presented their gifts to Negus, a day was set for the Muslims to meet Negus and confront the Meccan delegation. On the appointed day, Negus sat on the throne, surrounded by the priests and his retinue, in front of whom stood all the Meccans. The two Meccan delegates addressed him: 'Some foolish boys of ours have come to your country. They abandoned the faith of their people, yet they haven't converted to Christianity. We are sent by the nobles of our people so that you may return those boys to them.'

Negus asked the immigrants: 'What is this faith that made you abandon your people's religion and refuse to embrace our religion?' Jafar bin Abu Talib, Muhammad's cousin and Ali's brother, replied: 'Like the rest of our people, we used to worship idols until a messenger of us came and called for the worship of God alone, and leave idol worship. We believed in him and followed him. It is because of this that our people are oppressing us, in order to force us back to idol worship. That is why we had to leave our country and our people and come to Abyssinia, running away from oppression.'

When Negus asked them if they had with them anything that was brought by their Prophet, Jafar read to him a part of the Qur'anic Sura of Maryam (Mary). Negus and the priests in his court, greatly touched by these verses, began to shed tears. The king then denied Mecca's request to deliver the Muslims to the Quraysh, and said: 'These words, of what had descended on Jesus, come from the very same source as that of Jesus.'

Nevertheless, the next day Amr bin al-As, one of Mecca's two representatives, tried to play a trick. He claimed that the Muslims abused Jesus, saying that he was a slave of God. Negus then asked the immigrants: 'What do you say about Jesus son of Mary?' One of them answered: 'We say about him what our Prophet has brought us; he is the Servant of God, his messenger, his spirit and his work which he gave to Virgin Mary.' Negus picked up a rod and said: Go, you are free in my land. He then returned the Quraysh's gifts to their representatives, and they departed in shame.

The Muslim emigrants remained in Christian Abyssinia for many years, and indeed some did not return to their country until the Prophet himself migrated to Medina. They lived among the Christian people of Abyssinia, working, worshipping and living their normal life, in complete safety and freedom. While they managed to convert some Abyssinian Christians to Islam, some Muslim emigrants were also converted to Christianity.

According to Muslim tradition, when Negus died sixteen years later, Muhammad announced his death on the same day he died, and led his followers' prayer *in absentia* for the Abyssinian King, although he was a Christian. (Turmuzi's *Traditions: The Book of the Messenger of God's Funerals*, Chapter: What is mentioned about the Prophet's Prayer on Nagashi, Tradition 1039)

7

The Deaths of Khadija and Abu Talib

A few months after the migration of Muhammad's followers to Abyssinia, the Prophet gained an important supporter in Mecca. Hamza, Muhammad's uncle, a hunter who was regarded as the strongest man in Mecca, accepted Islam and later became known as the *Lion of God* because of his bravery. His conversion came about as a result of the hostility of Abu Jahl, one of Mecca's leaders, to his nephew Muhammad. Having returned from a hunting trip in the desert, Hamza went straight to visit the Kaaba, his bow slung over his shoulder. When he reached the Sanctuary, he heard that Abu Jahl had heaped abuse and insults upon his Muhammad. Outraged, Hamza dashed to the Sanctuary, where Abu Jahl was sitting with some leaders of Mecca, and began to beat him with his bow, shouting: 'Are you going to insult him now, now that I am of his religion?' As his companions stood warily, Abu Jahl cried out apologising and cowered at the feet of Hamza.

Soon after in AD 616, another important Meccan joined Muhammad. Umar ibn Al-Khattab, a powerful Quraysh leader, followed Hamza in converting to Islam. Umar had opposed Muhammad from the very beginning and strongly defended the traditional, polytheistic religious system of Arabia. He was most adamant and cruel in opposing the Prophet and very prominent in persecuting the Muslims. Umar had decided to get rid of the Prophet in order to put an end to his new faith. According to Islamic sources, Umar decided to kill Muhammad and, with the sword in his hand, went out looking for him. When, on his way, he was told that his own sister and her husband had converted to Islam, he decided to pay a visit to his sister first. After beating both his sister and her husband, he demanded to see the sheets of the Qur'an they were reading. When he has finished reading it, the story goes, Umar soon calmed down and asked to meet the Prophet to announce his own conversion.

While Muhammad and the few followers left in Mecca were celebrating the great event, the Quraysh were alarmed by the conversion of two of their strongest men. As insult and pressure had failed to persuade him to change his mind about their gods, the Quraysh tried to bribe the Prophet. According to Ibn Ishaq, Utba, who was one of their chiefs, said while sitting in a Quraysh assembly:

> 'Why don't I go to Muhammad and make some proposals to him? If he accepts, we will give him whatever he wants, and he will leave us in peace.' They thought it was a good idea . . . So Utba went to the Prophet, who was sitting in the mosque [at the Sanctuary] by himself, and said, 'O my nephew, you are one of us yet you have come to our people with a matter that is dividing the community. You are ridiculing our customs. You have insulted our gods and our religion. You have even declared that our forefathers were infidels. So listen to me, and I will make some suggestions, and perhaps you will be able to accept one of them.' The Apostle agreed. Utba said, 'If what you want is money, we will gather for you some of our property so that you may be the richest man in town. If you want honour, we will make you a chief so that no one can decide anything apart from you. If you want sovereignty, we will make you king.' [Ishaq:123]

Muhammad, however, was not interested in their offer, which made the Meccans more frustrated. They had no idea what else they could do to silence the enemy of their gods. At last they came to the conclusion that the only way to silence him was by forcing his clan to stop protecting him. As Abu Talib, his uncle was the leader of the Banu Hashim, they decided to punish Abu Talib and all his Hashemite clan and thereby force him to give up protecting the Prophet.

A few days before the end the lunar year in AD 616, forty Quraishi leaders met in Mecca's Town Hall on the instigation of Abu Jahl, the leader of the opposition, to decide what action they should take. They drafted a document which stipulated that unless the Banu Hashim surrendered Muhammad to them, they would be subjected to a social and economic boycott. The Quraysh decided to enter into a confederacy against the Hashemites; that they would not intermarry with them, that they would not sell or buy anything from them, and that all kinds of dealings with them should cease. The Quraysh leaders signed the ban document, which they fixed to the wall in the Kaaba.

Abu Talib stood fast, refusing to hand his nephew over, and rallied the whole clan of Banu Hashim behind him. However, on the first day of the lunar year in AD 617, realising the dangers ahead, Abu Talib decided to lead the Banu Hashim and the Banu al-Muttalib in an exodus from Mecca to a safer location in a valley between two mountains near the city. There were some natural defences and they lived there in a state of siege. It was entered on the city side by a low and narrow gateway, while on all other sides it was detached from Mecca by cliffs and buildings. Thus except for what they were able to carry with them during their departure, the Hashemites were cut off from their food and water supplies, as well as other necessities of life. The siege went on for three whole years, during which they went through much pain and suffered hunger and deprivation. Water was the most valuable item for the besieged clans during these three years, and they received it from Khadija, who paid the high price of smuggling water to feed their thirst.

Occasionally, the few friends that the Banu Hashim had in Mecca, such as Hakim bin Hizam, Khadija's nephew, who carried food and water to his aunt, and Hisham bin Amr Al-Aamiri, who also smuggled supplies into the ravine. He brought food and water for them as often as he could, a few hours before daybreak. Gradually, after three years of the siege, some members of Meccan society started to feel the injustice of their action and demanded an end to the siege. When they gathered at the Sanctuary to discuss the matter, five of Mecca's leaders publicly proclaimed their denunciation of the unjust boycott, and tore the infamous document of the Quraysh into pieces. At the end of the meeting, Mecca's leaders decided to abandon the siege, allowing the Banu Hashim and Banu al-Muttalib to return to their homes in the city in AD 619.

Although Mecca's boycott failed to force the Banu Hashim to withdraw their support for Muhammad, it did eventually succeed in removing their protection from the Prophet. Both Abu Talib and Khadija, who stood by him and gave him their support, came back from the mountain broken with ill health and no money. Khadija, who had spent all her life in luxury and comfort, was forced to spend three years in her old age living in a mountain hide-out, suffering from hunger and thirst, and enduring extreme heat in summer and cold in winter. At the same time, she spent all her wealth on water, food and clothing for the Hashemites. It was a time of excessive austerity for her, which inevitably took its toll. As a result, shortly after coming home in AD 619, Khadija, aged sixty-four, fell ill and died after twenty-four years of marriage. It was Muhammad himself who buried his wife, using one of his cloaks as a shroud, and it was he also who dug the grave and descended into the grave to lay her body before smoothing the earth on her grave.

The loss of his beloved wife, who had always believed in him and stood by him, came as a great shock for Muhammad. Waraqa's cousin had believed in his mission since he was just a young man, asked to marry him in order to protect him, and provided him with all the love and comfort he needed so that he would be ready on the day when he received his call. Khadija's death left Muhammad alone with nobody to comfort or support him and filled his heart with sorrow.

Around the same time as Khadija died, Muhammad's uncle also died. Abu Talib, who was in his eighties, had suffered much during the three-year siege. As a result, his health deteriorated soon after his return to Mecca. When it became known that he would not live long, some of the Quraysh leaders visited him. They said that if he managed to stop his nephew's attacks on their gods, they would leave the new religion alone. When Muhammad joined the meeting, however, he insisted that they should accept his monotheistic belief.

The Deaths of Khadija and Abu Talib

The deaths of Khadija and Abu Talib in the same year left Muhammad on his own against the Quraysh, as he now lost his clan's protection. 'It was then that the Quraysh began to treat him in an offensive way which they would not have dared to follow in his uncle's lifetime. A young lout actually threw dust on his head.' (Alexander Guillaume, *The Life of Muhammad* p. 191) Powerful Meccan leaders began to persecute Muhammad and his small band of devoted followers, whose new faith rejected the pagan core of Meccan cultural and economic life.

8

Journey to Heaven

Abu Talib was succeeded as the head of the Hashemite clan by Abu Lahab, another uncle of Muhammad, who completely opposed his nephew's actions and withdrew the clan's protection from him in AD 619. This threatened to put an end to both Muhammad and his religion. Now, it was not only the leaders of Mecca who attacked him; even young children hurled dust and insults at him. Muhammad soon realised that his hopes for Meccans to accept his call had been lost, and began to look for an alternative arena to preach his religion. Up to that time, about ten years after the start of his mission, only one hundred and seventy men and women had followed him in Mecca, and half of those had already migrated to Abyssinia. The first alternative location he though of was the city of Ta'if, seventy miles south-east of Mecca. Sometime before the end of AD 619, Muhammad left Mecca to go to Ta'if, hoping to find new followers there who could protect him against the aggression of his own people.

When he arrived at Ta'if, Muhammad was received by the three chiefs of the local tribes, who let him have his say freely. However, when he started asking them to abandon their gods and acknowledge Allah as the only deity, their welcoming mood changed, and they lost interest in his words. Nevertheless, Muhammad did not give up, but went on preaching his religion in their city. The chiefs became apprehensive lest his welcome in Ta'if might embroil them with the Meccans. So they left the street boys and the idlers of the town to deal with him. They greeted him with mockery and ridicule, before stoning him with clods and rocks, chasing him out of the city. Wounded and covered with blood, Muhammad staggered out of Ta'if and headed for home.

When he approached the city of Mecca, however, Muhammad

realised that his life would be in danger if he entered the city without protection. Now that he had lost the Hashemite support, Muhammad sent messages to other Meccan leaders, asking for their protection. Only one of them, Mut'im ibn Adi, agreed to provide safety for the Prophet and he sent his men to escort him into Mecca. Abu Jahl, the leader of the Quraysh's opposition to Muhammad, accepted Mut'im's protection, and it became safe for the Prophet to live in his city. Nevertheless, when he started to preach again in Mecca, he 'found that its people were more determined to oppose him and to abandon his religion, except for a few weak people who believed in him.' (Ibid., p. 194)] This was one of the darkest and most dismal moments in Muhammad's life, early in AD 620. Following his failure to gain any support at Ta'if, he now seemed to be rejected by his own people, who, but for the courageous intervention of Mut'im ibn Adi, might not have allowed him to enter Mecca at all.

Having failed to gain any new followers in Ta'if or Mecca, Muhammad now started to approach the other Arabian tribes visiting Mecca for pilgrimage, asking them to embrace his religion. He visited them at their dwelling places in the city to preach about his monotheistic belief: 'The apostle offered himself to the tribes of Arabs at the fairs whenever opportunity came . . . He used to tell them to believe in him and protect him until God should make clear to them the message with which he had charged his prophet.' (Ibid., p. 194) This attempt was also a complete failure. Not one of the tribes was ready to abandon its idol worship and follow Muhammad. It was in this darkest period of his life that Muhammad received support from a higher authority: he got an invitation to Heaven, from Allah himself.

In this desperate moment of his life, Muhammad went through a very special experience; known as *al-Israa'* and *al-Mi'raj* (the Night Journey). According to Islamic tradition, Muhammad made a two part journey during one night, during the first part of which he travelled from al Masjid al Haram (the Sacred Mosque) in Mecca to al-Masjid al-Aqsa (the Distant Mosque) in Jerusalem. From there, he went on the second part of the journey, ascending to Heaven until he had reached the throne of God.

It began with Muhammad resting in the Kaaba in Mecca, when the archangel Gabriel came to him in the latter part of night, with a winged horse, *Buraq*, which quickly carried them both to the Temple Mount in Jerusalem. There Muhammad met with earlier prophets – Abraham, Moses and Jesus – and led them in prayer. According to Muslim tradition,

> The apostle was carried by night from the mosque at Mecca to the Masjid al-Aqsa, which is the temple of Aelia [Jerusalem] . . . It was an act of God . . . to show him His signs . . . Buraq, the animal whose every stride carried it as far as its eye could reach on which the prophets before him used to ride, was brought to the apostle and he was mounted on it. His companion (Gabriel) went with him to see the wonders between heaven and earth, until he came to Jerusalem's temple. There he found Abraham the friend of God, Moses, and Jesus assembled with a company of the prophets, and he prayed with them. Then he was brought three vessels containing milk, wine, and water respectively. The apostle said: "I heard a voice saying when these were offered to me: 'If he takes the water he will be drowned and his people also; if he takes the wine he will go astray and his people also; and if he takes the milk he will be rightly guided and his people also.' So I took the vessel containing milk and drank it. Gabriel said to me: You have been rightly guided and so will your people be." [Ibid., pp. 181–2]

Following this experience, Muhammad remounted *Buraq* for the second part of the journey, which took him to heaven to see the signs of God. There Allah instructed him on the five daily prayers prescribed for Muslims. Muhammad is supposed to have said:

> I mounted the animal, and ascended until we arrived at the lowest heaven, and Gabriel demanded that the door should be opened . . . and when I arrived in the first heaven, behold, I saw Adam . . . and when I arrived in the second region, behold, I saw John (the Baptist) and Jesus . . . After that we went up to the third heaven and . . . I saw Joseph . . . After that Gabriel took me

> to the fourth heaven, and . . . behold, I saw Enoch . . . (And) Gabriel took me to the fifth heaven, and . . . I saw Aaron. And Gabriel took me to the sixth heaven, and . . . I saw Moses. And Gabriel . . . took me up to the seventh heaven . . . and behold, I saw Abraham . . . After that I was taken up to the tree called *Sidratul-Muntaha* (the Lote Tree); . . . And I saw four rivers there; two of them hidden, and two manifest. I said to Gabriel, "What are these?" He said: "these two concealed rivers are in Paradise; and the two manifests are the Nile and the Euphrates."
>
> [*Sahih Bukhari*, Volume 1, Book 8, Number 345;
> Volume 4, Book 54, Number 429;
> Volume 5, Book 58, Number 227;
> Volume 9, Book 93, Number 608;
> *Sahih Muslim Book* 001, Number 0309;
> Book 001, Number 0313.]

Thus Muhammad was able to reach the ultimate limit a man could reach, in the presence of God. For the Lote Tree represents the farthest boundary beyond which no one can travel, in their approach to God. The only mention of this tree in the Qur'an is found in chapter 53, An-Najm (The Star), regarding Muhammad's Journey to Heaven: 'So did Allah convey the inspiration to His Servant . . . Will ye then dispute with him concerning what he saw? For indeed he saw him at a second descent, Near the Lote-tree beyond which none may pass: Near it is the Garden of Abode.' (*The Meaning of the Glorious Qur'an*, translated by Abdullah Yusuf Ali, Nadim, London, 1976, verses 10, 12, 13, 14, and 15)

When Muhammad woke up the following morning, he told the story of his journey, which the Meccans regarded as absurd: 'The apostle returned to Mecca [in the same night] and in the morning he told the Quraysh what had happened. Most of them said, "By God, this is a plain absurdity! A caravan takes a month to go to Syria and a month to return, and can Muhammad do the return journey in one night?" Many Muslims gave up their faith.' (Alfred Guillaume, *The Life of Muhammad*, pp. 181–2)

While some interpreters regard this experience to be a physical journey, others consider it as a spiritual experience or vision. Imam Bukhari has a tradition from Ayesha that only Muhammad's spirit had journeyed to 'the distant place of prayer'. Some argue that the journey was a type of metaphor – a mode of revelation for Muhammad in symbolic form – while other traditions suggest that it was a physical journey.

Here we find a close similarity between the Islamic account of Muhammad's Journey to Heaven and the Jewish Apocalyptic account regarding Abraham's Journey to Heaven. According to *The Apocalypse of Abraham*, a Jewish pseudepigraphic book from the Old Testament whose claimed authorship is unfounded and which is considered to be part of the Apocalyptic or 'Revelation' literature, Abraham had a similar experience.

The third part of the Book of Abraham includes an account of the ascension of Abraham to heaven in almost exactly the same way as Muhammad. Terah, Abraham's father, was a maker of idols. When Abraham explained to his father the uselessness of the idols and objected to idol worship, Terah became angry with his son. Abraham then heard a voice from heaven, asking him to leave his father's house. Instead of Gabriel, Abraham was invited by another angelic character called Yahoel (Yahwe-Elohim) to mount a dove rather than a horse. Yahoel took Abraham and ascended to the heavens. When they reached the seventh heaven Abraham saw the throne of God. He saw the rivers and their origin, as well as the Garden of Eden and the Fall of Adam and Eve. Abraham then saw a scene of idolatry, with boys being slaughtered, and God explained that this was his Temple and his priesthood full of his anger against the people who followed Abraham. This was followed by a vision of the destruction of the Temple in Jerusalem, which, God explained, was due to the sin of idolatry on the part of his seed. (*The Apocalypse of Abraham* edited with a translation from the Slavonic text and notes by G. H. Box with the assistance of J. I. Landsman, Society for Promoting Christian Knowledge, London, 1918)

The al-masjid al-Aqsa mentioned in the account of Night Journey as Muhammad's destination in Jerusalem is not the same as the present day mosque of the same name. At the time of the

Night Journey in AD 621, there was neither a Jewish temple nor an Islamic mosque on Temple Mount of Jerusalem. In AD 70, the Romans destroyed Jerusalem and its temple; sixty years later, they rebuilt the city of Jerusalem, calling it Aelia Capitolina, which was occupied by a Roman colony. The new city was dedicated to the Roman deity Jupiter, to whom a temple was built on the site of the former Temple Mount, with a huge statue of the god inside of it. When Rome converted to Christianity in the fourth century AD, the Temple of Venus, to the west of the Temple Mount, was replaced by the Church of the Holy Sepulchre, and the Temple of Jupiter on the Temple Mount was torn down. Thus, in AD 621, when Muhammad experienced his Journey to Heaven, the area of the Temple Mount was a garbage dump. In the 630s, the Caliph Umar took the city of Jerusalem and in AD 715 the Umayyad Caliph al Walid built al-Aqsa Mosque in the southern section of the Temple Mount.

9

Banu an-Najjar Support their Cousin

After his miraculous Journey to Heaven, Muhammad's position became even worse than before. Not only was he unable to gain any new followers in Mecca, but many of the visiting Arab tribes would not even listen to him, while some of his own followers started to leave him. They dismissed his account of his Night Journey as unbelievable. Now, the Prophet's followers in Mecca became even fewer in number than before; some had fled to Abyssinia, and others had wavered and turned back, while those few who remained in Mecca were isolated and surrounded by great numbers of Quraishi. So weak and few in number were the Muslims in Mecca that they lived in continuous fear of being wiped out.

In this desperate situation, Muhammad had no hope of converting any more men of the Quraysh. Aware of the Prophet's enforced isolation and the irreconcilable opposition of Mecca to his cause, the other Arab tribes became all the more reluctant to receive his call. Despite his reliance upon Hamza and Umar, and his confidence that the Quraysh could no longer harm him, Muhammad saw that his followers, limited as they were to a small number of weak people, had become exposed to the danger of apostasy or extermination.

It was at this moment of desperation that an unexpected turning point took place, which changed his fortunes dramatically and gave him new hope of victory and success. As they had done before with his grandfather Abd al-Muttalib when he was oppressed by his people more than half a century ago, the Banu an-Najjar, his father's maternal cousins, came from Yathrib to support Muhammad. At the pilgrimage in the summer of AD 620, six men came from Yathrib; three from the Banu an-Najjar, Taym Allah of the clan of Bani Malik, As'ad bin Zurara known as Abu Umama, and Auf bin al-Harith. They met Muhammad and soon declared without argument or hesitation that they accepted his monotheistic message and regarded him as their prophet.

> When God wished to display His religion openly and to glorify His prophet and to fulfil His promise to him, the time came when he met a number of Helpers at one of the fairs; . . . he met (them) at al-Aqaba . . . they were of the Khazraj and allies of the Jews. He invited them to sit with him and expounded to them Islam and recited the Qur'an to them. Now God had prepared the way for Islam in that they lived side by side with the Jews, who were people of the scriptures and knowledge, . . . Thereupon they accepted his teaching and became Muslims.
>
> [Alfred Guillaume, *The Life of Muhammad*, pp. 197–8, paras 286–7]

Yathrib was not a strange city for Muhammad, as he had many close relatives in that city. As a young boy of six, Aamina, his mother, took him to visit his father's grave at Yathrib. On their way back to Mecca, his mother fell ill and died, and was buried midway between Yathrib and Mecca. Yathrib was the city of Salma, the great grandmother of Bani Hashim, and her family the Banu an-Najjar. When Abd al-Muttalib, Hashim's son and Muhammad's grandfather, was wronged by the Quraysh, it was the Banu an-Najjar who came to help him. Now they came once more to Mecca as Helpers of Hashim's great-grandson.

However, it is surprising that they embraced Muhammad's monotheistic belief quickly and without hesitation. Islamic historians ascribe their readiness to accept the monotheistic faith to their living among the Jews of their clan. Muhammad regarded Banu an-Najjar as the best of his followers in Yathrib, and is reported to have said: 'The best of the Ansar's families (homes) are those of Banu An-Najjar.' (Sahih Bukhari, *Merits of the Helpers (Ansar) in Medina*, numbers 133–5) These men, being related to Mohammed on his grandmother's side, took up his cause and were active on its behalf among their people.

The following year, in the summer of AD 621, five of the six Yathribites returned to Mecca, accompanied by another seven who had converted to Islam. They came to see Muhammad, whom they met at al-Aqaba in Mina near Mecca during the stoning of the devil ritual of the pilgrimage. This time, they made a formal declaration, pledging to abstain from idolatry, theft, and adultery; to tell no lies; to refrain from killing their infant daughters, which was the custom in Arabia; and to obey Muhammad in all good things. As we can see, this declaration included a list of religious and moral imperatives, similar to the Ten Commandments that were given to Moses on Mount Sinai. On their departure, Muhammad sent with them a reader who could teach them the Qur'an.

Back in Yathrib, these helpers of Muhammad established their own Muslim community which became known as the Ansar, and were the first to perform Friday Prayers, even before the Muslims of Mecca. Abu Umama and As'ad bin Zurara of the Banu an-Najjar were the first to gather forty of Muhammad's followers at Yathrib and lead them in Friday prayer, in a place called Naqi' al-Khadamat. (Ibn Hisham, *Assyra an-Nabawiya*, part 2, Cairo Dar al-Tawfiqiya, p. 24)

The Ansar Pledge their Alliance with Muhammad

The next year, in June AD 622, seventy-three men and two women came from Yathrib along with others who were as yet unbelievers. As they had already accepted Islam before coming to Mecca, this time they came with an invitation to Muhammad to leave Mecca and come to their city. Life was becoming too difficult for him in Mecca and Muhammad did not hesitate in accepting their invitation. Fearing the Quryash's reaction to this news, he met the Ansar in secrecy during the night at al Aqaba, accompanied by his uncle al-Abbas. Upon their professing their sincerity, the Prophet swore to be faithful to them, and they promised to defend him as they would protect their own wives and children, and if necessary to fight for his sake.

[They] gathered together in the gully waiting for the apostle until he came with his uncle al-Abbas who was at that time a polytheist; . . . The apostle spoke . . . and then said 'I invite your allegiance on the basis that you protect me as you would your women and children.' Al-Bara [the Ansar chief and senior] took his hand and said: 'By Him Who sent you with the truth, we will protect you as we protect our women. We give our allegiance and we are men of war possessing arms which have been passed on from father to son.' While al-Bara was speaking Abul-Haytham . . . interrupted him and said, 'O apostle, we have ties with other men (he meant the Jews) and if we sever them perhaps when we have done that and God will have given you victory, you will return to your people and leave us?' The apostle smiled and said: 'Nay, blood is blood . . . I am of you and you are of me . . . ' The apostle said, 'Bring out to me twelve leaders that they may take charge of their people's affairs.' They produced nine from al-Khazraj and three from al-Aws.

[Alfred Guillaume, *The Life of Muhammad*, pp. 203–4.]

Encouraged by his alliance with the Ansar, Muhammad started to persuade his Meccan followers to leave for Yathrib in small groups, and about seventy did so. They disappeared silently from Mecca and proceeded to Yathrib, where they were received with enthusiasm and much hospitality, until all the followers had left except Muhammad, Ali and Abu Bakr. They were accommodated in the homes of the Yathribites who had accepted Muhammad as a prophet.

Yathrib (Medina)

Yathrib was a fertile oasis more than two hundred miles (340 km) north of Mecca and about 120 miles (190 km) east of the Red Sea coast, in which date palms flourished and cereals were grown. It was a collection of scattered settlements surrounded by groves of date-palms and cultivated fields. The name Yathrib is apparently Egyptian, identical with the well known city-name Athribis (Atribi). The earliest mention of Yathrib dates back to the sixth century BC, when it appeared in the Chronicle of Nabonidus, the last king of

Babylonia, who settled in the oasis of Taima in northern Arabia. It was an important station on the caravan route between Hijaz and Yemen in the south and the Levant in the north.

The first people to settle the oasis of Yathrib were the tribe of Banu Matraweel and Banu Hauf, who trace their lineage to Shem son of Noah. In the second century AD, in the wake of the Jewish-Roman wars, some Jewish tribes came to settle in Yathrib. It seems probable that some were refugees from Palestine, perhaps men who left after the defeat of Bar Kokhba:

> When in AD 70 the Romans massacred the Jews in Palestine, and then in AD 132 expelled them from that land, many of the Jewish tribes fled to find an asylum in the Hijaz, a territory that was contiguous to Palestine in the south. There, they settled wherever they found water springs and greenery, and then by intrigue and through money lending business gradually occupied the fertile lands. Ailah, Maqna, Tabuk, Taima, Wadi al Qura, Fadak and Khaiber came under their control in that very period, and Bani Quraizah, Bani al-Nadir, Bani Bahdal, and Bani Qainuqa also came in the same period and occupied Yathrib.
>
> [Mawdudi, in his comments on Surah 59 of the Qur'an reporting from *Kitab al-Aghani*, vol. xix, p. 94, by Abu al-Faraj Ali of Esfahan (897–967)]

There were three prominent Jewish Tribes which inhabited the Yathrib, al-Nadir, Qurayza, and Kaynuqa, as well as eight clans which were distinguished among the Arabs. Then, around the mid-fifth century AD, a great flood in Yemen forced some tribes to migrate to other parts of Arabia, among which were the Aws and the Khazraj, who came to settle in Yathrib. For a time, these Yemeni immigrants were subordinate to the Jews; however, they soon gained their independence. Eventually, the Aws and the Khazraj became hostile to each other and Jewish tribes were also divided; while the Banu Nadir and the Banu Qurayza allied themselves with the Aws, the Banu Kaynuqa sided with the Khazraj. These two groups went on fighting for more than a century; their last battle was the battle took place about 618 AD, a few years before the arrival of Muhammad.

So at the time of Muhammad, Yathrib was divided into two Arab tribes, the Aws and the Khazraj, and three Jewish tribes, Banu Nadir, Banu Kaynuqa, and Banu Karayza. In addition, al-Samhudi lists about a dozen other Jewish groups, of whom the most important was the Banu Hadi. (Ali bin Ahmad al-Samhudi was an Islamic scholar, his best-known work *Wafa al-Wafa bi akhbar dar al-Mustafa*)

10

Muhammad's Nation

In September 622 AD, warned of a plot to assassinate him, Muhammad secretly slipped out of Mecca with his close friend and ally Abu Bakr. They left by night, and reached the outskirts of Yathrib about nine days later, on Monday the 12th of Rabi'ul-awwal, thirteen years after his call. The oasis was soon renamed Medina, meaning 'the City'. This was the *Hijra*, or 'emigration,' which has become the traditional starting point of Islamic history. The Islamic Era begins on the first day of the Arabic year in which the hijra took place: 16 July AD 622 in the Western calendar.

> After his companions had left, the apostle stayed in Mecca waiting for permission to migrate. Except for Abu Bakr and Ali, none of his supporters were left but those under restraint and those who had been forced to apostatise . . . When the Quraysh saw that the apostle had a party and companions [the Ansar] not of their tribe and outside their territory, and that his companions [of Mecca] had migrated to join them, and knew that they had settled in a new home and had gained protectors, they feared that the apostle might join them, since they knew that he had decided to fight them. So they assembled in their council chamber, the house of Qusai bin Kilab . . . to take counsel what they should do in regard to the apostle, for they were now in fear of him . . . The discussion opened . . . One advised that they should put him in irons behind bars . . . (However) Abu Jahl said . . . that each clan should provide a young, powerful, well-born, aristocratic warrior; that each of these should be provided with a sharp sword; then that each of them should strike a blow at him and kill him. Thus they would be relieved of him, and

> responsibility for his blood would lie upon all the clans . . .
>
> Before much of the night had passed they assembled at his (Muhammad's) door waiting for him to go to sleep so that they might fall upon him. When the apostle saw what they were doing he told Ali (his cousin) to lie on his bed and to wrap himself in his green Hadrami mantle; for no harm would befall him . . . The apostle (then) came out to them with a handful of dust . . . God took away their sight so that they could not see him . . . he came to Abu Bakr and the two then left by a window in the back of the latter's house and made for a cave on Thaur, a mountain below Mecca . . . [Later] When three days had passed and men's interest waned, the man they had hired came with their camels.
>
> [Alfred Guillaume, *The Life of Muhammad*, pp. 221–33]

On his arrival in Yathrib, Muhammad stayed for few days at Quba, just outside the city, among the Banu Amr bin Auf. He then left and went into the city looking for a location where he could settle. Although many of the clans he had passed by invited him to stay with them, his camel took him to the home of Banu Malik ibn an-Najjar. There among the Najjarites, his camel knelt at an area which was used by two young orphans as a drying-place for dates. Muhammad decided to build his residence and his mosque on that spot, and he stayed with Abu Ayyub bin Zaid until the building was completed.

Muhammad spent the first eighteen months in Medina settling down, while his house and mosque were being built. His house, adjacent to the new mosque, eventually held different apartments grouped around a central courtyard for each of his wives. Although during the early part of his life Muhammad married only one woman, Khadija, after her death he married about thirteen other women, but he had only nine wives at any one time. Following Khadija's death, in AD 620 Muhammad married Sawda bint Zama, who was about fifty-five years old, five years older than him. Soon after, while still in Mecca, he was betrothed to Ayesha daughter of his friend Abu Bakr, although their marriage took place in Medina three years later. As well as being the youngest (she was eighteen when he died in AD 632), Ayesha is also believed to have been the only virgin among his wives, the majority of whom were either divorcees or widows. Both Sawda and Ayesha joined Muhammad in Medina a short time after his migration and were given apartments adjoined to the new mosque in Medina.

Muhammad married the rest of his wives between the third and the seventh year after the Hijra. Among them were two Jewish women; Rayhana, who had been married to a man from the Jewish tribe of Banu Qurayza who was executed, and Safiyah daughter of Huyayy, the chief of the Jewish tribe of the Banu Nadir which was later expelled from Medina and migrated to Khaybar in north Hijaz. Muhammad also married a Christian woman, Mariya the Coptic slave from Egypt.

The community of believers

As soon as he had settled down, Muhammad set about the establishment of a pact known as the Constitution of Medina between the Immigrants who came from Mecca, his Ansar in Medina, and the Jewish tribes of the city. Conditions of the pact, according to traditional Muslim sources, included boycotting the Quraysh, abstinence from 'extending any support to them', and assistance of one another if attacked by a third party, as well as 'defending Medina in case of a foreign attack'.

According to the document that has been preserved, the Constitution of Medina creates a confederation on traditional Arab lines, between the clans of Medina and the emigrants from Mecca. Introducing the document, Ibn Ishaq states:

> The apostle wrote a document between the emigrants and the helpers, in which he made a friendly agreement with the Jews [of Medina] and established them in their religion and their property, and stated the reciprocal obligations, as follows: In the name of God the Compassionate, the Merciful. This is a document from Muhammad the Prophet [governing the relations] between the believers and the Muslims of the Quraysh and Yathrib, and those who followed them and joined them and

laboured with them. They are one community (*umma*) to the exclusion of all men. The Quraysh emigrants according to their present custom shall pay the blood wit within their number and shall redeem their prisoners . . .

The Banu Auf according to their present custom shall pay the blood wit they paid in heathenism; every section shall redeem its prisoners . . . Believers shall not leave anyone destitute among them by not paying his redemption money or blood wit in kindness . . . A believer shall not slay a believer for the sake of an unbeliever, nor shall he aid an unbeliever against a believer. [Both Muslims and Jews here are regarded as believers] . . . Believers are friends one to the other to the exclusion of outsiders. To the Jew who follows us belong help and equality. He shall not be wronged nor shall his enemies be aided . . . Whenever you differ about a matter, it must be referred to God and to Muhammad . . .

The Jews of Banu Auf are one community with the believers, the Jews have their religion and the Muslims have theirs . . . The same applies to the Jews of the Banu an-Najjar, Banu al-Harith, Banu Sa'ida, Banu Jushm, Banu al-Aws, Banu Tha'laba, and the Fafna, a clan of Tha'laba and the Banu al-Shutayba . . . The Jews must bear their expenses and the Muslims must bear their expenses. Each must help the other against anyone who attacks the people of this document. They must seek mutual advice and consultation, and loyalty is a protection against treachery . . . Yathrib shall be a sanctuary for the people of this document . . . If any dispute or controversy likely to cause trouble should arise, it must be referred to God and to Muhammad the apostle of God . . . The Quraysh and their helpers shall not be given protection. The contracting parties are bound to help one another against any attack on Yathrib . . . The Jews of al-Aws, their freedmen and themselves have the same standing with the people of this document in pure loyalty from the people of this document . . . God is the protector of the good and God-fearing man and Muhammad is the apostle of God.

With this document, Muhammad established a new community comprised not of blood ties but of spiritual brotherhood. The believers, both Muslims and Jews, formed one community, to the exclusion of outsiders. In addition to being a community or umma based upon faith, Medina was also a polity based upon the establishment of sacred territory, or *haram*. The emphasis on common religion and territory in the Constitution of Medina, however, should not obscure its continued recognition of pre-existing family and tribal relationships. In essence, the polity Muhammad sought to establish could be expressed in three iterations: a tribal polity, a territorial polity, and a religious polity. The Constitution did not form a political state but a federation of tribal clans; no central government, no tax, and no unified army. Other than stating that he was the prophet, according to this document Muhammad was given no special authority in the Community of Medina, except that serious disputes must be referred to him. Disagreements arising in the congregation were to be brought before Allah and His Apostle.

11

The Expulsion of the Jews

Although when he arrived in Medina in AD 622, Muhammad included the Jews of Yathrib in his *umma,* this situation did not last long. Within five years, the three main Jewish tribes, Banu Qurayza, Banu Nadir and Banu Kaynuqa, were forced to leave the city. Some of them were executed, their women and children enslaved. However, Islamic sources have nothing to tell us about the fate of the smaller Jewish clans of Medina, including Banu An-Najjar, and it is therefore assumed that they eventually embraced Islam and became part of the Ansar.

In March 624, during the second year of the Hijra, Muslims led by Muhammad defeated the Meccans of the Banu Quraysh in the Battle of Badr, which became a turning point in the early history of Islam. The battle, which took place south of Medina, was the first large-scale engagement between Muhammad's followers in Medina and the strong men of Mecca. As well as strengthening his position in Medina, Muhammad's victory in Badr was the first sign that he might eventually defeat his enemies in Mecca, and signalled other tribes that a new power had arisen in Arabia. However, shortly after his victory in Badr, Muhammad faced his first conflict with the Jews of Medina.

According to Ibn Ishaq, a dispute broke out between the Muslims and the Banu Kaynuqa when a Muslim woman visited a jeweller's shop in the Kaynuqa marketplace. The goldsmith, a Jew, pinned her clothing such that upon getting up, she was stripped naked. A Muslim man who came upon the resulting commotion killed the shopkeeper in retaliation. The Jews in turn killed the Muslim man, which escalated to a chain of revenge killings, and enmity grew between Muslims and the Banu Kaynuqa. This event was regarded by Muslims as a violation of the Constitution of Medina and accordingly, Muhammad decided to besiege the Banu Kaynuqa for fourteen or fifteen days, after which the tribe surrendered unconditionally. When Abdullah ibn Ubayy, one of the chiefs of the Khazraj clan, spoke out against them, Muhammad agreed to expel the tribe from the city. The Banu Kaynuqa left, going first to the Jewish colonies in the Wadi al-Kura, north of Medina, and from there to Der'a in Syria.

Following their defeat at Badr, the Meccans desired to avenge their losses and strike back at Muhammad and his followers. Led by Abu Sufyan ibn Harb, they marched out from Mecca towards Medina, and were met by the Muslim forces at the valley located in front of Mount Uhud, in Northwestern Arabia. The two armies fought on the slopes and plains of Mount Uhud on 19 March AD 625, in the third year of Hijra. In spite of their small numbers, the Muslims gained the early initiative and were able to force the Meccan lines back, thus leaving much of their camp unprotected. However, when the battle looked to be only one step away from a decisive victory, a serious mistake was committed by a part of the Muslim army. This shifted the outcome of the battle. The Muslim archers left their assigned posts to despoil the Meccan camp, allowing a surprise attack from the Meccan cavalry which brought chaos to the Muslim ranks. Seventy-four Muslims were killed in the fight, and Muhammad himself came out badly injured. While the Muslims were retreating up the slopes of Uhud, the Meccans marched back to Mecca declaring victory.

The Jews were especially jubilant about Muhammad's defeat, declaring that if he had claimed Badr to be a mark of divine favour, Uhud, by the same process of reasoning, must be a proof of disfavour. At the same time, the Banu Nadir decided to challenge the Prophet's authority in Medina. In the summer of the same year, two men were killed by an ally of the Jews during a skirmish in which the Muslims were involved. Muhammad went to the Nadir asking them to make a contribution towards the blood money of the two men killed, but they postponed the contribution until later that day. Muhammad then left their locality in a hurry, accusing them of plotting to kill him. He besieged the Banu Nadir, and ordered them to surrender their property and leave Medina within ten days, but they decided to resist. After a siege that lasted for fourteen days, the Banu Nadir was forced to surrender. Under the terms of surrender, they had to leave Medina within ten days, and could only take with them what they could carry on camels, with the exception of weapons. They left on six hundred camels, parading through the city to the music of pipes and tambourines. Al-Waqidi described their impressive farewell: 'Their women were decked out in litters wearing silk, brocade, velvet, and fine red and green silk. People lined up to gape at them.' (Marsden Jones (ed.), *Al-Waqidi*, 1966, Kitab al-Maghazi, London, pp. 363–75) After leaving Medina, most of the Banu Nadir settled among the Jews of Khaybar in northern Arabia, while others emigrated to Syria.

Two years later a new dispute started with the third Jewish tribe of Medina, the Banu Qurayza. Some of the Jewish exiles had stirred up the Quraysh and other Arab tribes to attack Muhammad, and persuaded the Banu Qurayza to join them in their plans. In 627 the Meccans, accompanied by tribal allies including Abyssinian mercenaries as well as the Banu Nadir, marched against Medina and laid siege. As the invading forces were much bigger than his own, Muhammad decided to dig a trench rather than face the tribes in the open. The trench, together with the city's natural fortifications, prevented the invaders' horses and camels from entering the city, and the two sides were locked in a stalemate. It was then that the Banu Qurayza, who were allies of the Aws, entered into secret negotiations with the besiegers, who persuaded the Qurayza to attack Medina's forces from the south. Mohammed, however, succeeded in making the Jews and their Arab allies suspicious of each other; and the allies who had been besieging Medina suddenly departed in the midst of a storm, thus leaving the Qurayza unsupported. Subsequently, the tribe Qurayza was charged with treason and besieged by the Muslims commanded by Muhammad.

On the day of the Meccans' withdrawal, Muhammad marched against them and laid siege to their fortress a few miles to the southeast of the city. Their fate was left in the hands of Sa'ad ibn Mu'adh, who, although of the tribe of Aws, the allies of the Qurayza, felt bitter toward them on account of their supposed treachery toward the Muslims. He decided that all the men should be killed, the women and children sold as slaves, and the property divided among the army. The next morning, the Banu Qurayza surrendered and the Muslims seized their stronghold and their stores. The men, numbering about 750, were bound and placed under the custody of Muhammad ibn Maslamah; while the women and children, numbering about 1,000, were placed under Abdullah ibn Salam, a former rabbi who had converted to Islam. Ibn Ishaq describes the killing of the Banu Qurayza's men as follows: 'They surrendered, and the apostle confined them in Medina in the quarter of . . . a woman of B. al-Najjar. Then the apostle went out to the market of Medina and dug trenches in it. Then he sent for them and struck off their heads in those trenches as they were brought out to him in batches . . . There were six or seven hundred in all.' (Alfred Guillaume, *The Life of Muhammad*, pp. 461–4) Thus the last of the powerful Jewish tribes in Medina was destroyed.

Some modern commentators have condemned the execution of the Jews of Medina, and their expulsion from their homes. Of course, according to our modern standards of moral behaviour, this tragic end of the Jews of Medina is unacceptable. Nobody in our modern times would agree to the killing of people, whoever they were, even if they had committed a serious crime like that of which the Jews of Medina were accused. Today most civilised countries have even abolished capital punishment altogether. However, during the time of Muhammad the situation was different, not only in Arabia but all over the world. In a similar situation, Moses himself, the great Israelite leader, is reported to have ordered the killing of many more Israelites than the seven hundred executed in Medina.

Exodus 32 relates that the Israelites, anxious about Moses' prolonged absence on top of Mount Sinai, demanded that Aaron provide a god to lead them. Aaron collected the golden ornaments of the people and fashioned the gold into the shape of a calf or a small bull. The image was hailed by the people as a representation of the God who had brought Israel out of Egypt. Aaron then built an altar, and on the following day sacrifices were offered and the people feasted and danced and played. When Moses, carrying the Tablets of the Ten Commandments, came down from the Mount, he saw the Israelites dancing around the golden calf. On that day he decided to punish the calf-worshippers among the children of Israel: 'And the children of Levi did according to the word of Moses: and there fell of the people that day about three thousand men.' (Exodus 32:28)

12

Who were the Ansar?

Now, we need to know more about those Ansar who came to Muhammad from Medina when he had failed to gain followers among his own people in Mecca with open hearts, and accepted his teaching without doubt or hesitation. The usual explanation we get from Islamic sources is that their readiness to accept Islam was due to Jewish influence: 'Now God had prepared the way for Islam in that they (the Ansar) lived side by side with the Jews, who were people of the scriptures and knowledge . . . Thereupon they accepted his teaching and became Muslims.' (Alfred Guillaume, *The Life of Muhammad*, p. 198) This explanation, however, is unconvincing: from the first instance Medina Jews themselves have rejected Muhammad's message. Indeed, had these Ansar been influenced by the Jewish teaching, they would certainly have rejected Muhammad's message.

If it was true that the Arab inhabitants of Medina became ready to embrace Islam as a result of their close contact with the Jewish tribes there, then why did those same Jews reject Muhammad? As soon as the Prophet came to Medina in AD 622, he met with the undisguised hostility and ridicule of the Jewish community there. While the Arab inhabitants of Medina, the tribes of Aws and Khazraj, all joined Islam within two years of the Hijra, the monotheistic Jews of the city not only rejected Muhammad's religion but even went as far as to ally themselves with the polytheists of Mecca in order to get rid of him.

Although we do have records of the fate of the three main Jewish tribes of Medina – the Banu Qurayza, Al-Nadir, and Kaynuka – nothing more regarding the fate of the other smaller Jewish clans is mentioned in the Constitution of Medina; that is to say the Jews of Banu Auf, Banu an-Najjar, Banu al-Harith, Banu Sa'ida, Banu

Jushm, Banu al-Aws, and Banu Tha'laba. What happened to these Jewish clans of Medina who were part of the Arab tribes, and why is there no record of them after Muhammad's death? The answer is obvious: these Arabian clans, including their Jews, embraced Islam and became part of the Ansar in Medina.

While attacking the three Jewish tribes of Medina, Muhammad himself was living among the Banu an-Najjar, including their Jews, who stood by him and supported his actions. Moreover, the Prophet of Islam himself assumed the leadership of Banu an-Najjar a short time after his arrival in Medina:

> When Abu Umama died [during the months in which the mosque was being built] the Banu an-Najjar came to the apostle, for Abu Umama was their leader, saying that he held the high rank the apostle knew of and would he appoint someone from them to act in his place; to which the apostle replied, 'You are my maternal uncles, and we belong together so I will be your leader.' . . . Henceforth the Banu an-Najjar regarded themselves as highly honoured in having the apostle as their leader. [Ibid., p. 235]

If Muhammad was preaching a monotheistic religion similar to theirs and accepted the Law of Moses their leader, why then did the rabbinic Jews oppose him? If we examine the evidence carefully we find that the main reason for those Jews to reject Muhammad's message was that it included some elements which completely contradicted their own beliefs. From the very start of his mission in Mecca, Muhammad's message included two main elements: monotheistic belief in one God without an image; and the belief in the Last Day, including the resurrection of the dead and the final judgment. The conception of the last judgment – a doctrine that stands at the centre of early Islamic preaching – is connected in the most intimate fashion with faith in one God, belief in his unlimited power, and the consciousness of his moral essence which men are to keep before them as a model. All these ideas, which appeared already in the first Meccan period, are rooted in the grand cyclical conception of revelation. While the one God was the centre of Jewish belief, the resurrection of the dead was at the core of

Christian religion. Muhammad believed in the Law of Moses as well as the resurrection of Jesus, whom he regarded as the Christ. Here, although agreeing with the Rabbinic Jews on the unity of God, Muhammad completely contradicted them in his belief of the Last Day. The idea of resurrection and last Judgment was the core of Christian belief and the New Testament, but had nothing to do with the Old Testament. The Rabbinic Jews did not believe that Jesus was either a Messiah or prophet.

'When Muhammad came to Medina he met with the undisguised hostility and ridicule of the Jewish community there . . . Muhammad soon . . . attacks them for being insufficiently concerned with the impending judgement day: "if the abode of the world-to-come with God were reserved to you to the exclusion of all other men, then, if ye were speaking the truth, ye should long for death". (2:94)' (Chaim Rabin, *Qumran Studies*, Oxford University Press, 1957, p. 125) According to Ibn Hisham, some Jews of Medina came to Muhammad and asked him:

> . . . about the (earlier) apostles he believed in. So the apostle said: 'We believe in God and what he has sent down to us and what was sent down to Abraham and Ishmael and Isaac and Jacob and the tribes [of Israel] and what was given to Moses and Jesus and what was given to the prophets from their Lord; we make no difference between any one of them. And we are submissive unto Him.' When he mentioned Jesus, Son of Mary, they denied that he was a prophet, saying, 'We do not believe in Jesus, Son of Mary, or in anyone who believes in him.' . . . So God sent down concerning them: 'Say, O Scripture folk (People of the Book), you have no standing until you observe the Torah and the Gospel and what has been sent down concerning you from your Lord.'
>
> ([Alfred Guillaume, *The Life of Muhammad*, p. 268]

If the three main Jewish tribes of Medina opposed Muhammad and his teachings, the Ansar must, then, have been influenced by another kind of Jew who favoured the prophet. This indicates that the Jews of Medina were not all the same; while the three main tribes of Banu al-Nadir, Banu Qurayza, and Banu Kaynuqa represented the Rabbinic orthodox teaching, some clans such as Banu an-Najjar, which were attached to and Aws, followed a different kind of Judaism. What ki would have been ready to accept Muhammad's teaching, e in regard to the resurrection of the dead and the Last D ve must also bear in mind that as well as the great majority of Jews who followed rabbinic Judaism, which was regarded as the orthodox and right path, there was a minority who accepted Christianity and became known as Judeo-Christians. These Jews, like Muhammad, regarded Jesus as a prophet, but denied his divinity.

The Essenes

It is certain that the Banu an-Najjar did not represent the rabbinic form of Judaism and that although they were part of the Jewish community as a whole, they were ready to accept Muhammad and his teachings. The Banu al-Najjar made up the majority of those who first went to meet Muhammad in Mecca and accept his religion, and it was also they who gave him a site on their land to build his mosque and his residence in Medina. Moreover, Muhammad was related to the Banu al-Najjar through his grandfather. Hashim, Muhammad's great-grandfather, had married Salma daughter of Amr, a woman of the Najjar clan who bore him his son Abd al-Muttalib, Muhammad's grandfather.

Chaim Rabin, associate professor of Hebrew language at the Hebrew University of Jerusalem, suggests that those Jews of Medina who came into contact with Muhammad while he was still in Mecca before the Hijra were 'anti-Rabbinic Jews' related to the Essenes of Qumran and the Dead Sea Scrolls: Arabia was the obvious place for a group from the neighbourhood of the Dead Sea to flee to. The desert regions of Transjordan and the northern Hijaz were home to several Judeo-Christian sects, and 'Arabia' was known to the Church Fathers as *ferax 'haereseon* (fertile in heresy). On the other hand, they were not the only Jews in the Peninsula. There was the large community in the Yemen and the village dwellers of the Wadi 'al-Qura, as well as the prominently Aaronid city of Medina. These were Rabbinic Jews, and relations can hardly have been good. (Chaim Rabin, *Qumran Studies*, p. 129)

Although the majority of the Jews of Palestine refused to accept Jesus as their Messiah, a small number of them did accept him and followed his teachings. These Jews, who believed in Jesus whilst remaining part of the Jewish community, became known as the Essenes, and they lived in a small community by the Dead Sea. They believed in the monotheistic faith of Moses but accepted the resurrection of the dead on the Day of Judgment. The Essenes were a Judeo-Christian sect which flourished in Palestine from about the second century BC to the end of the first century AD. Until the discovery of their library, *The Dead Sea Scrolls,* in caves at Qumran in 1947, the Essenes were known only from Greek sources (that is, sources written in Greek).

According to the accounts given by Josephus, Philo of Alexandria, and Pliny the Elder, they clustered in monastic communities that generally excluded women. Property was held in common and all details of daily life were regulated by officials. The Essenes were never numerous; Pliny fixed their number at some four thousand in his day. They observed the Law of Moses, the Sabbath, and ritual purity. They also professed belief in immortality and divine punishment for sin. Josephus explained in his writings that, in complete contrast to the Old Covenant of Moses, which was simply to 'keep my Commandments' and which made no promise of eternal life, members of the Essene sect believed in immortality:

> It is firm belief among them that, although bodies are corruptible, and their matter unstable, souls are immortal and endure for ever; that, come from subtlest ether, they are entwined with the bodies that serve them as prisons, drawn down as they are by some physical spell; but that they are freed from the bonds of the flesh, liberated, so to speak, from long slavery, then they rejoice and rise up to the heavenly world.

at the Saviour – their Teacher of Righteousness – suffered and died, and they awaited his Second

However, the fate of the Essene community remai Following the Roman destruction of the city of Jerusa Temple in AD 70, the Diaspora of the Jews started. They le to settle in different parts of the Roman Empire. As ther elements of the Essene community anywhere in the Roman pire, scholars were persuaded to believe that the Essenes must have disappeared without a trace. There is indication, however, to show that the Essenes survived and, together with other rabbinic elements, crossed the Jordan River east to the Nabatean kingdom of Transjordan, before moving south to northern Hijaz in modern Saudi Arabia.

When we examine the life and beliefs of the Essenes, we find many similarities with both the Hanifs of Arabia and the Ansar of Medina. Muhammad himself was given to solitude and meditation on the barren rocky hills outside Mecca, like the Essenes of the Dead Sea. He frequently retired to seek relief in meditation amongst the solitary valleys and rocks near Mecca, and used to spend some time in a cave in mount Hira. There he would retire for days at a time, and there he spent the whole month of Ramadan every year, engaged in some form of religious devotion similar to the Essenes. After the first encounter with the angel Gabriel, Muhammad had no other visions for three years, after which period the angel announced to him that he has been chosen by God to be his messenger. Three years is the time span required by the Essenes to allow a new member to join the community.

The Essenes considered themselves the guardians of the Divine Teaching, the light that shines in the darkness and invites the darkness to change itself into light. They shunned Temple worship and were content to live ascetic lives of manual labour in seclusion. After a year's probation, proselytes received their Essenian emblems but they could not participate in common meals for two more years. They condemned slave-owners and did not hoard silver and gold. On the seventh day they abstained from work and proceeded to the holy places. Members of the sect began their day with prayer, followed by purification rituals and a communal meal. They then did their work, mostly farming the land for food, and prayed again at sunset before coming together for an evening meal. Their *Community Rule,* one of the documents found at Qumran, says that the Council of the Community should include twelve men.

As we saw earlier, while Muhammad eventually got rid of the three rabbinic tribes, the small Jewish clans who were attached to Arab tribes remained in Medina and became part of the Ansar, who followed Muhammad and fought for him against their own people. The reason they accepted Muhammad's teaching so readily is that they belonged to the Essenes, who regarded him as the prophet they were waiting for. His Islamic teaching agreed completely with their Judeo-Christians beliefs. 'The Qumran sect . . . has numerous connections both with the early Church and the Judaeo-Christian sects. Thus features common to it, Islam, and one of the foregoing can provide such a connection has been made probable by traits common to the Qumran sect and Islam alone.' (cf. B. Reicke, *N. T. Studies*, i, 1954, pp. 137–41) According to Chaim Rabin, associate professor of Hebrew language at the Hebrew University of Jerusalem, the type of Judaism represented in Arabia during the time of Muhammad was that of anti-rabbinic Jews following in the same tradition as the Qumran community. Chaim believes that some late remnants of the Qumran sect survived in Arabia until the seventh century AD. (Chaim Rabin, *Qumran Studies*, p. 112)

Like the Qumran literature, the Qur'an makes extensive use of the symbolism of light and darkness to distinguish between the realms of God and Satan: 'Allah is the light of heavens and earth . . . Allah guides to His light whom He wills . . . as to those who disbelieve, their deeds are like . . . darkness upon a vast abysmal sea, layer upon layer of darkness . . . and he for whom Allah has not appointed light, for him there is no light.' (Sura 24:35–40). This symbolism also exists in the New Testament, which even uses the Qumran term 'children of light', (Luke xvi, 8; Eph. v, 8; I Thess. v, 5) . . . Like the Qumran sect and the New Testament, Muhammad held the entire Old Testament, prophets and all, to be books of prediction.

> An important difference between the [Dead Sea] Scrolls and Rabbinic Judaism is that the latter knows of an evil force within man, the 'evil inclination', while the Qumran sect, like Christianity, the Mandaeans, and some late midrashim . . . know only of an external Satan who misleads men into sin. This, of course, is the position of Islam too. Possibly a polemic against the doctrine of the internal duality in man is reflected in the statement, Kuran, Sura 33:4, in the wake of a rather obscure reference to divorce and adoption, 'Allah has not given man two hearts.' [Chaim Rabin, *Qumran Studies*, p. 122]

We can now understand why so many of Muhammad's attacks against the Jews of Medina can be paralleled from the New Testament.

Thus the Jews are frequently accused of slaying the prophets wrongfully. This, of course, also occurs in the New Testament . . . Indeed, such arguments in both New Testament and Qur'an may have preserved much which by accident has not been preserved amongst the fragments of the Qumran literature available to us. In a number of passages Muhammad holds up his Jewish partisans as an example of the Medinean Jews. We may expect to learn from these something of their identity from Sura 3:110: ' . . . If the people of the book (Jews and Christians) believed, it would be better for them, but some of them are believers and most are evildoers.' We thus learn that the 'believers' were few in comparison with the mass of the Jews, . . . we learn further from Sura 10:93; 45:17: the Jews 'did not differ until the knowledge came to them'. While other groups always claimed to preserve the pristine purity (orthodoxy) of Judaism, the Qumran sect ascribed its *halakhah* (Jewish religious law) to the new revelation of 'hidden things concerning which all Israel had gone astray . . . '

It is those Jews who 'have the knowledge' who accept Muhammad's claim (17:108), saying, 'the promise of our Lord is indeed carried out' – i.e. Muhammad is the 'gentile prophet' expected . . . only a 'group' (*fariq*) distorts scripture (3:78; 4:45) . . . As against these, there is 'among you a community (*umma*) that calls to that which is right' (3:107); 'and of the people of Moses, there is a community who guide rightly (or are rightly guided) with truth and thereby become just' (7:159); 'They are not the same as a community among the people of the book who stand and read the verses of God part of the night, while prostrating themselves, who believe in God and in the last day . . . they are the upright' . . . (*as-salihuna*) reminds one that the Hebrew equivalent, *yesharim*, appears practically as a name of the Qumran sect. (Ibid., pp. 126–7)

13

Christians in Arabia Before Islam

During the time of Muhammad, in the sixth and seventh centuries AD, Christianity had already spread into most Middle Eastern countries; to Egypt, the Levant and some border areas of Iraq, and in Ethiopia in east Africa. In Arabia, as well as some scattered Christian families in different parts of the Arabian Peninsula, there was a considerable Christian community in the area of Najran. They had established themselves there by the mid-fourth century, a century and a half before the birth of Islam. These Christians were known as *Nsara*. While the New Testament books refer to Jesus himself as being the 'Nazarene', 'belonging to the City of Nazareth' in Galilee, the Arabs used to call the followers of Christ *Nasara*, the singular of which is *Nasrani*, from the root 'Nasara', which means 'helped or granted victory'. This same expression in Hebrew, '*Nasrani*', was also used by the Jews to indicate 'a Christian'. Later, Muhammad, who seems to have looked at Jesus' experiences as a prototype of his own mission, called his own followers in Medina the *Ansar*, i.e. 'Helpers'.

Najran is a city in south-western Saudi Arabia near the frontier with Yemen, which was known in ancient times as al-Ukhdood. It was an important stopping station on the Incense Route between Yemen and the north, as well as being a centre of cloth making, arms manufacture and leather production. When confrontation began between Dhu-Nuwas, the king of Yemen who had embraced Judaism, and the emperor of Christian Abyssinia across the Red Sea, Dhu-Nuwas retaliated by attacking the Christian community in Najran, killing many of them and burning some alive. As a result, the emperor decided to send his army to punish Dhu-Nuwas in Yemen. Abyssinian troops soon captured the Yemen, killed Dhu-

Nuwas and a large number of his people, and ordered the building of Christian churches. It was at the time of this attack on Yemen that Muhammad was born in Mecca, and this episode was later narrated in the Qur'an under the title of 'the story of Ukhdood', where the Yemeni attack was condemned.

By the time Muhammad started preaching for Islam during the early years of the seventh century, the Najran community had already become the largest Christian community in Arabia, with a highly organised religious life. No contact was made between the prophet of Islam and the Najran Christians until about two years before his death, when he had already become the master of Arabia.

In AD 628, Muhammad and his followers marched to Mecca, attempting to enter the city for pilgrimage, but were not allowed in. However, both Muslims and Meccans concluded a treaty whereby Muslims would be allowed into the city the following year. Two years later Mecca surrendered to Muhammad, who declared amnesty for the inhabitants and gave generous gifts to the leaders of the Quraysh. When Muhammad returned to Medina, the whole Arabian Peninsula, including Najran, came under his Islamic umbrella.

The prophet sent a representative to Najran, inviting its inhabitants to convert to Islam. The Christians of Najran responded by sending their own delegation to meet Muhammad in Medina:

> A deputation from the Christians of Najran came to the apostle [in Medina]. There were sixty riders, fourteen of them from their nobles of whom three were in control of affairs, namely (a) the *Aqib* the leader of the people, a man of affairs, and their chief adviser whose opinion governed their policy, Abdul Maseeh by name; (b) the Sayyid, their administrator who saw to transport and general arrangements, whose name was al-Ayham; and (c) their Bishop, scholar, and religious leader who controlled their schools, Abu Haritha ibn Alqama, one of Banu Bakr ibn Wail. Abu Haritha occupied a position of honour among them, and was a great student, so that he had an excellent knowledge of their religion . . . when they came to Medina they came into the

apostle's mosque as he prayed the afternoon prayer, clad in Yamani garments, cloaks, and mantles . . . The time of their prayers having come, they stood and prayed in the apostle's mosque, and he said that they were to be left to do so. They prayed to the east . . . The first three named above spoke to the apostle. They were Christians according to the Byzantine rite (Catholics), though they differed among themselves in some points, saying He (Jesus) is God; and He is the son of God; and He is the third person of the Trinity, which is the doctrine of Christianity . . .

When the two divines spoke to him, the apostle said to them, 'Submit yourselves.' They said, 'We have submitted.' He said: 'You have not submitted, so submit.' They said, 'Nay, but we submitted before you.' He said, 'You lie. Your assertion that God has a son, your worship of the cross, and your eating pork hold you back from submission.' They said, 'But who is his father, Muhammad?' The apostle was silent and did not answer them. So God sent down concerning their words and their incoherence the beginning of the *sura* of the Family of Imran, up to more than eighty verses . . .

When there came to the apostle news of Jesus from God and a decisive judgement between him and them, and he was commanded to resort to mutual invocation of a course if they opposed him, he summoned them to begin. But they said: 'O Abul Qasim, let us consider our affairs; then we will come to you later with our decision.' So they left him and consulted with the *Aqib* who was their chief adviser and asked him what his opinion was. He said: 'O Christians, you know right well that Muhammad is a prophet sent (by God) and he has brought a decisive declaration about the nature of your master (Jesus) . . . If you decide to adhere to your religion and to maintain your doctrine about your master, then take your leave of the man and go home.' So they came to the apostle and told him that they had decided not to resort to cursing and to leave him in his religion and return home.

[Alfred Guillaume, *The Life of Muhammad*, pp. 270–3, 277]

e we see that, contrary to present day preachers of political , who regard them as unbelievers, Muhammad not only allowed the Christian delegation to perform their prayers in his own mosque; he also accepted their decision to preserve their own faith and worship, at a time when he had already become the master of Arabia. This meeting between Muhammad and the Najran Christians shows that, although the two sides still had some theological disagreements, they were still able to accept each other and live together in peace, without accusations or hatred on either side.

Before their departure from Medina, Muhammad signed a treaty with the chiefs and Bishops of the Najran delegation:

> This is the pact which has been issued by the prophet Muhammad, peace be upon him, to the people of Najran, to whom his ruling shall extend – their fruit, their gold and silver money and their slaves. All these are left to them except the payment of 2,000 garments [each year], . . . They shall have the protection of God and the guarantee of Muhammad, the apostle of God, and they shall be secured [in] their lives, property, lands, creed, those [of them who are] absent and those present, their buildings, and their churches. No bishop or monk shall be displaced from his parish or monastery, and no priest shall be forced to abandon his priestly life. All their belongings, little or much, remain theirs . . . They shall not be called for military service, nor shall they pay tithe nor their land be transversed by [our] army. Those who seek justice shall have it: there will be no oppressors nor oppressed at Najran . . . For the continuation of this pact, the guarantee of God and the assurance of Muhammad, Apostle of God, sanction what has been written until God manifests his authority, so long as the people of Najran remain faithful and act in accordance with their obligations.
>
> [Al-Baladhuri, Ahmad ibn Yahyi ibn Jibir, *Futuh al-buldan*, p. 76; *Kitab alamwal*, p. 272]

14

Jesus in the Qur'an

With some minor differences, the Qur'anic story of the birth of Jesus agrees with the account of the New Testament gospels. While the Jews have refused to accept Jesus as their Messiah, the Qur'an regards him as a prophet, and accepts him as the Christ. However, the Qur'an has not accepted the belief in the trinity – Father, Son and Holy Ghost, three in One – and neither does it accept the claim of some Israelites that they killed and crucified Jesus. In general, there is no doubt that the Christians do believe in the unity of God, as the trinity for them does not indicate multiplicity, but rather represents one divinity. In contrast, the ancient Egyptian trinity has three different characters: Osiris the father, Isis the mother and Horus the son. There are those who explain the Christian trinity in the same way as the ancient Egyptians: the Lord, Mary and Jesus, but this explanation does not agree with the accepted teaching of Christianity.

The main role of Jesus (Iesa in the Qur'an) as portrayed in the gospels, concerns the fact that he was the Lord's Messenger, who came as a light for the nations: 'I am the light of the world: he that followeth me shall not walk in darkness, but shall have the light of life.' (John 8:12) He is also the redeemer who suffers in sacrifice like the lamb in order to redeem his nation's sins. He says: 'I am the good shepherd: the good shepherd giveth his life for the sheep.' (John 10:11)

Regarding his birth, Luke says:

> The angel Gabriel was sent from God . . . To a virgin espoused to a man whose name was Joseph, of the house of David; and the virgin's name was Mary. And the angel came in unto her, and

> said: Hail, thou that art highly favoured, the Lord is with thee: blessed art thou among women. And when she saw him, she was troubled at his saying, and cast in her mind what manner of salutation this should be. And the angel said unto her, Fear not, Mary: for thou hast found favour with God. And, behold, thou shalt conceive in thy womb, and bring forth a son, and shalt call his name Jesus. He shall be great, and shall be called the Son of the Highest: and the Lord God shall give unto him the throne of his father David: And he shall reign over the house of Jacob for ever; and his kingdom there shall be no end. [Luke 1:26–33]

The Qur'an tells us that Iesa (Jesus) was born of the virgin Maryam (Mary), who had not been touched by a man, as God had breathed into him of His Spirit. So the Messiah – according to the Qur'an's account – is the only human, who was born of God's Spirit: 'And Mary the daughter of Imran, who guarded her chastity; and We breathed into her (body) of Our spirit; and she testified to the truth of the words of her Lord and of His Revelations, and was of the devout (servants).' (66:12)

The Qur'an always refers to Jesus as 'Son of Mary', and cites the good news brought by the angels of his birth on the Virgin Mary: 'Behold! The angels said: 'O Mary! Allah giveth thee glad tidings of a Word from Him: his name will be Christ Jesus.' (3:45)

The titles of Jesus

The Qur'an describes Christ as 'Word of Allah' (Sura 3:45), 'His (God's) word' (4:171), 'a spirit of Him' (4:171). The Qur'an also says that God supported Jesus 'With the Holy Ghost' (2:87; 253 and 5:110) The Qur'an further mentions that God, to Whom be ascribed all perfection and majesty, brought Jesus 'Clear signs'. (2:87; 253) He gave him 'The Gospel' (57:27), and made him 'Blessed' wherever he was. (Sura 19:21) The Qur'an mentions that Jesus performed some miracles no man would be able to do. (3:49; 5:110)

As it appears in the New Testament gospels, the story of Christ says that Jesus was born in Bethlehem during the reign of Herod the Great, who ruled the land of Palestine for forty years and died in the fourth year BC. After his birth, his mother Mary escaped to Egypt with her child, fearing for his life. As the prophecies had warned him of the time and place of Christ's birth, who would claim the throne of David, King Herod ordered all children in Bethlehem to be killed. Mary only returned from Egypt with her son after Herod's death, when she went to live in the city of Nazareth in north Galilee.

According to the gospels, when Jesus was thirty, he went to the Jordan Valley where he met with John the Baptist, who baptised him with water in the middle of the river Jordan. Following that, Jesus retired to the desert for forty days. There he had a confrontation with the devil who, in trying to lure him, offered to make him king of the world. This attempt failed and Jesus returned to Galilee to choose his twelve disciples and begin his mission. Christ's very high teachings included the love of all people, even enemies. He said: 'Whoever of you who has no sin, let him throw her with a stone', 'Love your enemies' and 'Do unto others as you would have them do unto you'.

Christ's teaching provoked the hatred of the Jewish Sadducee priests and Pharisee Rabbis. According to the gospels, the priests became angrier when Jesus came to Jerusalem during Passover, entered the Temple and began preaching, which challenged their authority. They conspired against him and sent guards to capture him while he was resting with his disciples at the Mount of Olives north of the city, with the help of Judas Iscariot who betrayed him.

The investigation and trial in front of the Priests' Council headed by Caiaphas went on all night. In the morning, when the trial had ended, the priests took Christ to Pontius Pilate the Roman Governor of Palestine, who tried him again. Pilate unsuccessfully tried to free Jesus, as he found no reason to punish him; he then washed his hands to disavow his responsibility for crucifying him. The head priests instigated the masses' demands that Jesus should be crucified, and the Roman governor submitted to their desire. The gospel story ends with the resurrection of Christ on the third day, when his body disappeared from the tomb where it was placed. Later, he appeared to his disciples to ask them to spread the

Christian teachings among the nations, and he was raised to heaven after forty days.

The Christian Bible includes two parts: The Old Testament, which contains Moses' Torah as well as the historical books, the books of the Prophets and the psalms; and the New Testament, which contains the gospels, the Acts of the Apostles and the Apostles' letters, especially those of St Paul, to the early churches. As the Jews were mainly interested in the Torah and Talmud, it was the Christians who collected the books of the Bible in a canon. The word 'gospel' means 'good news' regarding the birth of Christ, however the gospels were written by the evangelists. Although at the beginning of the Christian era there were many gospels, the Church rejected most of them as being heretical, so the New Testament has only four: those of Matthew, Mark, Luke and John.

Christ the saviour who redeems mankind

The Jews have refused to accept Jesus as their Christ, and they are still waiting for the coming of their Messiah. The word 'Messiah' or 'Christ' had not been found in the Semitic languages, as it was not known by the Israelites during their early history. It is a word of Egyptian origin. Egyptians were the only people among the ancient peoples who anointed their kings with oils and perfumes at the time of their coronation. One of the ointments they used was crocodile fat, a custom still practised in Nubia, as they believed it produced strong progeny. Having been anointed with this fat, the new king would be given the title 'Messiah', written in hieroglyphic with two crocodiles. The word 'crocodile' in ancient Egyptian was 'meseh', so two crocodiles read 'meseeh'. Thus, in the beginning the word Messiah was used to indicate a king, which was the titles of all Egyptian pharaohs. The Hebrew scribes of the Old Testament started to use this title for the Israelite kings, starting from Saul and David, around the tenth century BC.

What has reached us of the Mosaic teaching in the Bible and the Qur'an only spoke about the unity of God, and had nothing to say about eternal life. Although there is a strong Jewish belief, as found in the teaching of Moses, in the unity of God and abandoning the worship of idols, this does not involve the spirit or the resurrection of the end of days. This was why the Sadducee priests rejected the idea of the resurrection of the dead. The Jews were waiting for the arrival of their Messiah, who would defend them against their enemies and make them the chosen people to rule the world under his leadership. The Hebrew expression *ha-melikh ha-masheekh* (the anointed king), is used for the expected Messiah of the Jews, who would be one of David's descendants. Thus, in its early usage, the title 'Messiah' had nothing to do with the Saviour.

However, when Jesus's followers started to believe in his resurrection, the word 'Messiah' got a new meaning; the 'Saviour' who promises eternal life. The idea of salvation had attracted mankind since ancient times, and the centre point of salvation had always been resurrection and eternal life. The essence of the Christian creed is the belief in the resurrection at the end of days and the final judgment. The main reason why the Jewish tribes of Medina refused to accept Muhammad's call was his acceptance of Jesus as the Messiah, the resurrection of the dead and the final judgment.

Christ is the word of God and a spirit of His

In the Qur'anic Sura 4:171, we find: 'Christ Jesus the son of Mary was an apostle of Allah and His Word, Which He bestowed on Mary and a Spirit proceeding from Him.' It is clear from this verse that Jesus Christ son of Mary is himself regarded as the Apostle of God and His Word. In Sura 3:45, we also find: 'Behold! The angels said: "O Mary! Allah giveth thee glad tidings of a Word from Him: his name will be Christ Jesus, the son of Mary, held in honour in this world and the Hereafter and of (the company of) those nearest to Allah".'

Christ in the Qur'an, then, is 'a Word of God', and a 'spirit of God', yet he is 'not the son of God', neither is he represented by a 'Trinity'. He is also the 'Messiah' (Christ), and the 'Messenger of God'. The phrase 'Word of God' has appeared in the Qur'an to indicate, either the words of the Qur'an itself, as we find in Sura

7:158; 'So believe in Allah and His Apostle, The unlettered (or Gentile) Prophet, who believed in Allah and His Words'. The same meaning is also expressed in Sura 2:75; 'A party of them heard the Word of Allah (the Qur'an), and perverted it.' Sura 16:102 talks about the revelation of the Qur'an saying: 'Say, the Holy Spirit has brought the revelation from Thy Lord.' The Word of God, indicating Christ, is also found in the New Testament: 'In the beginning was the Word, and the Word was with God, and the Word was God.' (John 1:1)

In spite of this, some Muslim scholars claimed that the expression 'Word of God', has nothing to do with the Divine Spirit, and instead take it to indicate the angel Gabriel. With regard to 'His Word which He bestowed on Mary', Ibn Kathir claims that 'His Word', rather than referring to God's Word, refers to the angel Gabriel. This interpretation also takes the 'Sprit of God' to mean Gabriel, which clearly contradicts the meaning of the Qur'anic text. The Qur'an says: 'Christ Jesus the son of Mary was an apostle of Allah and His Word.' So, whose word is it? It is God's Word. The verse goes on to describe Christ: 'A Spirit proceeding from Him (God).' The Qur'an here makes it clear that Jesus Christ was born of the Spirit proceeding from God himself, not from Gabriel. In Sura 3:45, 'The angels said: "O Mary! Allah giveth thee glad tidings of a Word from Him: his name will be Christ Jesus." ' So it is clear here that the angels – and Gabriel was one of them – gave Mary the news, not the spirit.

Imam Al-Razi explained the verse 'a Spirit proceeding from Him':: 'This is God's Spirit, as it is God who gives life to the world.' Imam Al-Baydawi explained the same verse phrase by saying that Christ was a spirit, because he was able to raise the dead.

The Qur'an makes it clearer when it says: 'To Jesus the son of Mary We gave Clear (Signs), and strengthened him with the Holy Spirit.' (2:253) Ibn Hishan explained that 'the Holy Spirit' in this verse is the Great Name (the name of God), with which Jesus was able to raise the dead. Abu Ja'far Arrazi said of Arrabi'a bin Anas that the Holy Spirit means the Lord, to Whom be ascribed all Perfection and majesty. Zamakhashri said: 'Having a spirit from cates that Jesus was near God.'

Christ's Miracles

Jesus is acknowledged in the Qur'an to have performed many miraculous actions, including curing the sick, those who were blind or lamed, casting out devils and raising the dead, even creating life:

> Then will Allah say: O Jesus the son of Mary! Recount My favour to thee and thy mother. Behold! I strengthened thee with the Holy Spirit, so that thou didst speak to the people in childhood and in maturity. Behold! I taught thee the Book and Wisdom, the Law and the Gospel. And behold! Thou makest out of clay, as it were, the figure of a bird, by My leave, and thou breathest into it, and it becomes a bird by My leave. And thou healest those born blind and the lepers by My leave. And behold! Thou bringest forth the dead by My leave. [5:110]

One of Christ's miracles mentioned in the Qur'an is not found in the New Testament. It is said that, after Mary has given birth to Jesus at a location away from her family:

> At length she brought the (babe) to her people, carrying him (in her arms). They said: 'O Mary! Truly an amazing thing has thou brought! O sister of Aaron! Thy father was not a man of evil. Nor thy mother a woman unchaste!' But she pointed to the babe. They said: 'How can we talk to one who is a child in the cradle?' He (Jesus) said: 'I am indeed a servant of Allah: He hath given me revelation and made me a prophet; and He hath made me blessed wheresoever I be, and hath enjoined on me prayer and Charity as long as I live: (He) hath made me kind to my mother, and not overbearing or miserable; So Peace is on me the day I was born, the day that I die, and day that I shall be raised up to life (again)!' Such (was) Jesus the son of Mary: (it is) a statement of truth, about which they (vainly) dispute. [19:27–34]

Christ the servant of God

One of the most important of Jesus' titles in the Qur'an is 'Abdullah', (The Servant of God). This had also been the title of the expected redeemer spoken of by the Israelite prophets. The Qur'an says: 'Christ disdaineth not to serve and worship Allah.' (Sura 4:172) The prophet Isaiah, who lived in the mid-eighth century BC, had spoken about the Suffering Servant: 'Behold my servant, whom I uphold; mine elect, in whom my soul delighteth; I have put my spirit upon him: he shall bring forth judgment to the Gentiles.' (42:1) and: 'And he said, It is a light thing that thou shouldest be my servant to raise up the tribes of Jacob, and to restore the preserved of Israel: I will also give thee for a light to the Gentiles, that thou mayest be my salvation unto the end of the earth.' (49:6).

Again:

> All we like sheep have gone astray; we have turned every one to his own way; and the Lord hath laid on him the iniquity of us all. He was oppressed, and he was afflicted, yet he opened not his mouth: he is brought as a lamb to the slaughter, and as a sheep before her shearers is dumb, so he openeth not his mouth. He was taken from prison and from judgment: and who shall declare his generation? For he was cut off out the land of the living: for the transgression of my people was he stricken. And he made his grave with the wicked and with the rich in his death; because he had done no violence, neither was any deceit in his mouth. Yet it pleased the Lord to bruise him; he hath put him to grief: when thou shalt make his soul in offering for sin, he shall see his seed, he shall prolong his days, and the pleasure of the Lord shall prosper in his hand. He shall see of the travail of his soul, and shall be satisfied: by his knowledge shall my righteous servant justify many; for he shall bear their iniquities. [Isaiah 53:6–11]

The same title, Servant of God, has also appeared in the Old Testament referring to a prophet or a king. 'Mine elect', used by Isaiah for the Servant, was also used for Moses and David. Thus we see that the title Abdullah, 'Servant of the Lord', had a special position in the Scripture, as it is given to kings and prophets. On the other hand, the expression 'I have put my spirit upon him' (Isaiah 42:1), is the same as the Qur'anic expression 'spirit of God'.

15

Mecca Surrenders to the Prophet

Just a few years after moving to Medina, Muhammad had managed to establish himself as a major power in Arabia, capable of challenging its great centre in Mecca. Soon after his confrontation with the Quraysh, the Prophet began to establish alliances with nomadic tribes in different parts of the Arabian Peninsula. At first he concluded non-aggression pacts with the tribes, but later as he became stronger he made it a condition that the allied tribes should convert to Islam. On the other hand, Mecca's position as the leading power and the religious centre of Arabia was threatened as a result of the spread of Islam and the growing strength of Muhammad. As a result the Quraysh became worried about their position as a trade centre as well as the safety of their trade route to the Levant in the north. The Meccans decided to resort to force in an attempt to weaken Muhammad's position before it would be too late for them to deal with him. Several battles followed the siege of Medina but Mecca's hopes were shattered as Muhammad was able to win or hold his own against their superior forces in all these battles.

The treaty of Hudaybiya

Realising his own strength, Muhammad took the initiative in challenging the Quraysh on their own ground. In 628, about a year after the Battle of the Trenches, he set out for Mecca to perform *umrah* (the little pilgrimage), accompanied by seven hundred of his followers and seventy camels for sacrifice. On his way, he called together the neighbouring Bedouins to join him, to make it difficult for the Quraysh to prevent him from visiting the Kaaba temple.

When the news reached Mecca about Muhammad's approaching caravan, the Quraysh sent out a force of two hundred cavalry to stop them reaching the city. However, Muhammad evaded them by taking a small, rugged, rocky track between passes, which led directly to of al-Hudaybiya, below the city of Mecca, where he camped. Soon negotiations commenced, with emissaries going between Mecca and Hudaybiya; these resulted in a ten-year treaty being signed between the Muhammad and the Quraysh. The main points of the treaty included the cessation of hostilities between the two sides; an agreement to repatriate any Meccan who had gone to Medina without the permission of his protector; and allowing the Muslims to make a pilgrimage to Mecca within the following year. This treaty was further cemented by Muhammad's marriage to Umm Habiba, daughter of Abu Sufyan, Mecca's leader.

After signing the truce of Hudaybiya Muhammad returned to Medina, where he stayed for less than two months, before marching out again against the Jewish oasis of Khaybar in the north. As the Banu Nadir, whom he expelled from Medina four years earlier had settled in Khaybar, 150 kilometres (95 miles) from Medina, and was inciting the neighbouring Arab tribes against him, Muhammad decided to silence them. The Jews of Khaybar eventually surrendered and were allowed to live in the oasis on the condition that they would give one half of their produce to the Muslims. Muhammad chose to marry Safiya, one of the Jewish captives, whose husband had died in the war.

According to Muslim tradition, it was also during this period that Muhammad sent letters to some world rulers, asking them to convert to Islam. Hence he sent messengers to Heraclius of the Byzantine Empire, Khosrau ruler of Persia, the chief of Yemen and to some others.

End of peace treaty

Two years after the truce of Hudaybiya, the Banu Bakr, who were allies of the Meccans, violated the peace treaty by attacking Banu Khuza'ah, who had good relations with Muhammad. Following this attack, Muhammad sent a message to the Meccans allowing them three options: to pay blood money for those slain among the Khuza'ah tribe; to disavow themselves of the Banu Bakr; or to declare the truce of Hudaybiya null. Still feeling superior, the Meccans accepted the last option, ending the truce with Muhammad. However, soon they realised they had made a mistake and sent their leader Abu Sufyan to Medina to try and renew the Hudaybiya treaty. Muhammad rejected all his father-in-law's pleas.

After visiting his daughter Umm Habiba, Abu Sufyan met the Prophet and was asked by al-Abbas, Muhammad's uncle, to accept Islam and testify that there is no God but Allah and that Muhammad is his apostle. Although Abu Sufyan was ready to accept that Allah is the only deity, he was still not sure about Muhammad being his prophet. Muhammad then told Abu Sufyan to return to Mecca and tell the people there that he would enter their city the next morning. Nevertheless, before leaving Medina, al-Abbas suggested to the Prophet that as Abu Sufyan was a proud man, it would be better to give him an honourable position among his people. Muhammad took his advice, and told Abu Sufyan, 'Tell the people that when we enter, anyone seeking refuge in your house will be safe.' In addition, the Prophet told him to assure the Meccans that those who remained in their own homes or at the Kaaba would also be safe. Back in Mecca, Abu Sufyan informed the Quraysh of Muhammad's plan to come to Mecca with a large army and suggested that it was best for them to surrender and remain safe in their homes.

The conquest of Mecca

In January 630, soon after Abu Sufyan's departure from Medina, Muhammad marched on Mecca with 10,000 men. It was in the fasting month of Ramadan eight years after his miraculous escape from Mecca that Muhammad was able to return to his home city. He entered Mecca without fighting as the leaders of the Quraysh yielded to him with virtually no resistance, and the city was taken with almost no loss of life. As soon as Muhammad entered Mecca, he got off his camel, bowed down on the ground and thanked Allah for this victory. Although a few years earlier the leaders of Mecca had been united in their plan to kill him, Muhammad declared an amnesty for past offences, except for ten men and women who had mocked and ridiculed him in songs and verses; even these were later pardoned.

Feeling safe, Meccans began to leave their homes and run to meet the Prophet at the Kaaba. When they arrived there, they found Muhammad performing the tawaf, the ritual of encompassing the Kaaba seven times, on his camel, touching the black stone with a stick in his hand. Having finished his ritual, he addressed the Meccans: 'O Quraysh, what do you think I am going to do to you?' They replied, 'You will treat us as a kind nephew and a generous brother would.' To this Muhammad said: 'God forgives you and He is the Most Merciful of the Merciful.' He then turned to the Kaaba. Pointing his staff at the three hundred and sixty-five idols which were placed there, he recited from the Qur'an: 'Truth has come and falsehood has vanished away. Lo! Falsehood is ever bound to vanish.' (17:8)

Muhammad then proceeded to purify the Kaaba, declaring it to be the sacred temple for all Muslims, and he ordered the removal of the idols that were kept there. Muhammad pointed at every one of the idols with a stick in his hand, ordering that all the images placed around the Kaaba should be collected, burned with fire and broken up. However, it is important to note that the apostle ordered that all pictures should be erased except those of Jesus and Mary. According to Al Azraqi the early Meccan historian, the Prophet said 'erase every image except which is under my hand', and then raised his hand off a picture of Jesus and his mother Mary. (Muhammad bin Abdullah bin Ahmed Al Azraqi, *Mecca's News*, Dar Al Andalus, Beirut, 1983) Though he did not insist on their becoming Muslims, most Meccans later converted to Islam and Muhammad subsequently destroyed all the statues of Arabian gods in and around the Kaaba.

Arabia becomes Muslim

Soon after the conquest of Mecca, Muhammad moved along the road to Ta'if, and defeated the Hawazin and Thaqif tribes in the Battle of Hunayn, before marching north on an expedition against Tabuk in northern Arabia and receiving the submission of some of the regional chiefs. Meanwhile, many Bedouin tribes submitted to Muhammad in order to be safe from his attacks and to benefit from the booties of the wars. At the beginning of the ninth year, on his return from Jirana, The Mosque of the Holy Prophet was now the scene of frequent embassies from all quarters of Arabia. From the most distant parts of the peninsula, from Yemen and Hadramaut, from Mahra, Oman and Bahrain, from the borders of Syria and the outskirts of Persia, the tribes hastened to offer submission.

However, the Bedouins maintained their independence, their established code of virtue and their ancestral traditions. Muhammad thus required them to refrain from attack on the Muslims and their allies, and to pay the *Zakat*, the Muslim religious levy. By the time of his death two years later, most of Arabia had been converted to Islam.

> During the last two years of his life, the Prophet had received the submission of most of the tribes of Arabia. This did not, of course, mean that the peninsula constituted a political unity, governed and administered from Medina. Submission involved two actions only: a nominal adherence to the Muslim religion and the payment of an annual tax. When Muhammad was alive, there was no government and no paid army. What revenue came into Medina was immediately distributed to the poor.
>
> [John Glubb, *A Short History of the Arab Peoples*, Hodder and Stoughton, 1969, p. 42]

Although Mecca had now fallen under his control, Muhammad did not want to return to his home city, preferring to remain among the Ansar in Medina. It appears that he did not even visit his old house, not far from the Kaaba.

16

The Farewell Sermon

Following Mecca's fall into Muslim hands in AD 630, pilgrimage to the city was instituted as an Islamic obligation. In March of the following year, at the end of the tenth year after the migration to Medina, Muhammad carried out his first truly Islamic pilgrimage, accompanied by tens of thousands of Muslim men and women. He showed his followers the rites of the annual Pilgrimage and taught them the customs of their *Hajj*. After completing the rituals, Muhammad delivered a famous speech known as The Farewell Sermon, in which he said: 'I do not know whether I shall ever meet you in this place again'. He also abolished all old blood feuds and disputes based on the former tribal system, and asked his male followers to be good to their women; for they are powerless captives in their households. Following this Sermon the last verse of the Qur'an is believed to have been delivered to the Prophet, stating: 'Today I have perfected your religion, and completed my favours for you and chosen Islam as a religion for you.' (Sura 5:3). This confirms that Islam as a religion became complete at that moment, before the Prophet's death, and no future changes could be allowed.

Muhammad's Illness

Having delivered his last sermon in Mecca, Muhammad returned to Medina. Two months later in the middle of the night, he went to the cemetery, where he prayed for the dead. The following morning, his sufferings began. Muhammad fell ill with a high temperature, headache and general weakness, yet he continued to lead prayers for eleven days. Instead of moving from one wife to another, Muhammad remained in Ayesha's apartment for the remaining days of his life. Ayesha daughter of Abu Bakr was the youngest and most loved of Muhammad's wives. Early in the second week of his sickness, his temperature soared and he fainted. They seated him in a container used for washing and poured water on him to cool his body. Although he felt well enough to move to his mosque next door and talk to people, he seems to have been expecting the end of his life. However, as he was approaching his death, he was worried about the future of the Ansar, his relatives who protected him and his cause until he was able to spread Islam all over the Arabian Peninsula. He told the followers who gathered in the mosque: 'I admonish you to be good to Al Ansar, for they are my family and with them I found shelter.'

Soon after this sermon, his last in the mosque, Muhammad became so weak that he could not move, so he asked his friend and father-in-law, Abu Bakr, to lead the prayers. About two weeks after he became ill, Muhammad died on 8 June, AD 632 at the age of sixty-three. He died on his bed in the arms of his beloved wife Ayesha, who was about eighteen at the time. All his children had died before him except Fatima, who died six months after him, while his wives remained widowed for the rest of their lives.

The Prophet's body was left at the same spot where he had died locked in Ayesha's room for about twenty-four hours, while his companions were busy trying to choose a successor. On the following day, his body was washed with his clothes on then shrouded in three white cotton cloths. (*Sahih Bukhari*, 1/169; *Sahih Muslim*, 1/306) Late that night, they dug a hole in the ground under his bed and buried him there. His burial place in Ayesha's apartment became part of Muhammad's mosque in Medina, where millions of Muslims now visit him every year.

Later in the day, when the news of Muhammad's death spread in Medina, there was confusion in the city. Some, including Umar ibn Al Kahttab, could not believe that the Prophet was dead. But Abu Bakr, who had visited Ayesha his daughter after Muhammad's death and seen his body, came to the mosque and addressed the congregation: 'O People! He (among you) who worships Muhammad, Muhammad is dead. But he who worships God, He is ever living and He never dies.' He then recited the Qur'anic verse 3:144: 'Muhammad is no more than an Apostle: many were the Apostles that passed away before him. If he died or were slain, will you then turn back on your heels? If any did turn back on his heels, not the least harm will he do to Allah; but Allah will swiftly reward those who (serve Him) with gratitude.'

17

Western Views of Muhammad

More than thirteen centuries after his departure, Muhammad is still regarded as one of the most controversial figures of world history. For over a millennium after his death in Medina, the image of Muhammad in the West remained highly negative, and it has only recently began to change. The first information to reach the West about the Arabian prophet came from the Levant. John of Damascus, a Levantine Christian monk who was born less than half a century after Muhammad's death and served as a Chief Administrator to the Muslim Caliph of Damascus, wrote a critique of Islam in Greek, known as *The Heresy of the Ishmaelites*. In this work, John described Islam as a heretical form of Christianity, a view that survived almost until modern times. In this book, which was later translated to Latin, John of Damascus says:

> There is . . . the superstition of the Ishmaelites which to this day prevails and keeps people in error, being a forerunner of the Antichrist. They are descended from Ishmael, [who] was born to Abraham of Agar, and for this reason they are called both Agarenes and Ishmaelites. They are also called Saracens, which is derived from Sarras kenoi, or destitute of Sara, because of what Agar said to the angel: 'Sara hath sent me away destitute.' [99] These (Ishamaelites) used to be idolaters and worshipped the morning star and Aphrodite, whom in their own language they called Khabár, which means great. [100] And so down to the time of Heraclius (the Byzantine Emperor) they were very great idolaters. From that time to the present a false prophet named Mohammed has appeared in their midst. This man, after having chanced upon the Old and New Testaments and likewise, it seems, having conversed with an Arian monk, [101] devised his

own heresy. Then, having insinuated himself into the good graces of the people by a show of seeming piety, he gave out that a certain book (the Qur'an) had been sent down to him from heaven. He had set down some ridiculous compositions in this book of his and he gave it to them as an object of veneration.

He says that there is one God, creator of all things, who has neither been begotten nor has begotten. [102] He says that the Christ is the Word of God and His Spirit, but a creature and a servant, and that He was begotten, without seed, of Mary the sister of Moses and Aaron. [103] For, he says, the Word and God and the Spirit entered into Mary and she brought forth Jesus, who was a prophet and servant of God. And he says that the Jews wanted to crucify Him in violation of the law, and that they seized His shadow and crucified this. But the Christ Himself was not crucified, he says, nor did He die, for God out of His love for Him took Him to Himself into heaven. [104] And he says this, that when the Christ had ascended into heaven God asked Him: 'O Jesus, didst thou say: "I am the Son of God and God"?' And Jesus, he says, answered: 'Be merciful to me, Lord. Thou knowest that I did not say this and that I did not scorn to be thy servant. But sinful men have written that I made this statement, and they have lied about me and have fallen into error.' And God answered and said to Him: 'I know that thou didst not say this word.' [105]

There are many other extraordinary and quite ridiculous things in this book which he boasts was sent down to him from God. But when we ask: 'And who is there to testify that God gave him the book? And which of the prophets foretold that such a prophet would rise up?' – they are at a loss . . . And we say that all the Prophets from Moses on down foretold the coming of Christ and how Christ God (and incarnate Son of God) was to come and to be crucified and die and rise again, and how He was to be the judge of the living and dead. Then, when we say: 'How is it that this prophet of yours did not come in the same way, with others bearing witness to him? And how is it that God did not in your presence present this man with the book to which you refer, even as He gave the Law to Moses, with the people looking on and the mountain smoking, so that you, too, might have certainty?' – they answer that God does as He pleases. 'This,' we say, 'We know, but we are asking how the book came down to your prophet.' Then they reply that the book came down to him while he was asleep. Then we jokingly say to them that, as long as he received the book in his sleep and did not actually sense the operation, then the popular adage applies to him (which runs: You're spinning me dreams.) [106]

Middle Ages

The view predominantly represented in the learned mediaeval West followed John of Damascus in regarding Islam as a Christian heresy, while the representation of Muhammad as part of the pantheon of a polytheistic Islam was a persistent element of the 'popular' image of Islam in the Middle Ages. The essential starting-points for the traditions about Muhammad which were circulating during this period were Byzantium on the one hand, and the Christians in Spain living under Islamic domination on the other. The early Byzantine knowledge about Muhammad and Islam became known in Europe in the ninth century through Anastasius Bibliothecarius, the Roman Catholic librarian who copied an earlier book by Theophanous, the eighth-century Byzantine monk, who had access to early Islamic-Arabic tradition. The most important source of information, however, was without doubt Spain.

Mediaeval traditions about Muhammad's experience of his call and his early preaching are dominated by the fact that his transition to prophethood is both proved and qualified as based on deception. The tendency to make Muhammad appear as a deceitful impostor who received instructions of his heretical teachers was prominent. The most favourite mediaeval theme seems to have been that of Muhammad the impostor, driven by ambition and eagerness for power and provided with magical qualities. 'Throughout the Middle Ages and well into modern times, Christianity judged Islam in a bleak manner, often grotesquely distorted. Not until the Enlightenment did the image of Islam start to change.' (Heribert Busse, *Islam, Judaism, and Christianity*, Markus Wiener, 1999, p. 1)

The Enlightenment

The concepts of the period of the Enlightenment permitted a more just estimate of Muhammad's personality. The thinkers of this period often elevated the outstanding wisdom and virtue of ancient lawgivers and founders of religions, and stressed the reasonableness of alien faiths, praising them at the expense of Christianity. They extended to Islam this benevolent evaluation of the non-Christian religions.

In his *Essai sur les moeurs* (1756), one of his most important works, Voltaire appreciated Muhammad as a conqueror, lawgiver, ruler and also as a priest. Voltaire's positive judgement found its way to Turpin's biography of Muhammad in three volumes (1773–9), which was then admitted by the English historian Edward Gibbon (*History of the Decline and Fall of the Roman Empire*, 1776–87).

Since the nineteenth century, thanks to the work of the orientalists, the first serious attempt of Europe to understand Islam has begun. However, although they no longer regarded him as an impostor, nevertheless the orientalists denied that he was a prophet. They believed that the Qur'an was a book written by Muhammad himself, rather than having been revealed to him, and that the religion of Islam was established by the Prophet himself. In his book *The Life of Mahomet* (1878), William Muir claims that Islam is Muhammad's own inspiration and argues that he became convinced that his own thoughts were God speaking to him, and so came to believe that every word of the Qur'an came directly from God. Although Muir does not deny Muhammad's spiritual experiences, he still insists on calling his claim of divine authorship a forgery.

The first biography of Muhammad which combined an endeavour towards historical accuracy with a positive appreciation of both Muhammad's personality and of Islam was written by the Frenchman Henri de Boulainvilliers. Boulainvilliers wrote a *Life of Mohammad* (London, 1730) with the avowed purpose of demonstrating the superiority of Islam to Christianity. He portrayed Muhammad as a wise and enlightened lawgiver, who sought to establish a reasonable religion in place of the dubious dogmas of Judaism and Christianity.

This same attitude is expressed in Claude Étienne Savary's translation of the Qur'an into French. Published in 1783, it was accompanied by an informative biography of Muhammad which attempted to be unbiased and testified to the growing interest of the Enlightenment in comparative religion. Although Savary refused to call Muhammad a prophet, he regarded him as one of those unusual personalities occasionally appearing in history, who remake their environment and enlist men in their triumphant train.

Modern times

New popular interest in Muhammad and Islam appeared in the West during the nineteen sixties and seventies. Here interest was more focused on the early part of Muhammad's life, during which he lived like a hermit, meditating in the desert. There was also great interest in the spiritual teachings of Sufism, which represents the inner, mystical dimension of Islam. However, this new popular interest in Islam and its Prophet soon came to an end with the victory of the Islamic revolution in Iran. In 1979, Grand Ayatollah Ruhollah Mousavi Khomeini, the Iranian Shi'a religious leader, overthrew Shah Reza Pahlavi, and ruled the country as the guardian of jurisconsult. Khomeini, who was regarded as the new face of Islam in Western popular culture, supported violent political Islam, taking hostages before issuing a religious *fatwa* calling for the assassination of the British author Salman Rushdie. The new Iranian leader, regarded in the Middle East as a champion of Islamic revival, inspired fear and distrust in the West. The American magazine *Time*, which in January 1980 named Khomeini Man of the Year, described him as a fanatic.

Soon after the Islamic revolution in Iran, al-Qa'ida, a new fundamentalist Sunni group sprang up, calling for global jihad. It attacked civilian as well as military targets all over the world, the most notable being the 11 September attacks on New York and Washington DC in 2001. People in the West saw young Muslim boys and girls blow themselves up in order to kill innocent people whom they didn't even know. On television, they watched Osama bin Laden, the leader of al-Qa'ida, and his chief Lieutenant, Ayman el-Zawaheri, praising the terrorists for the killings, all in the name of Islam and Muhammad its prophet.

Today, when talking about the prophet of Islam and his teaching, many Western people associate Muhammad with the images of Bin Laden, Zawaheri and Khomeini, who all call for jihad and the killing of innocent people in order to achieve the victory of Islam. On 30 September 2005 the Danish newspaper *Jyllands-Posten* published twelve editorial cartoons, most of which depicted the Prophet Muhammad as a fanatic terrorist with a sword or a gun in his hand. The newspaper announced that this publication was an attempt to contribute to the debate regarding criticism of Islam and self-censorship. In spite of the objection of Danish Muslim organisations to the publication of the cartoons, further examples of them were soon reprinted in newspapers in more than fifty other countries. This led to protests across the Muslim world, some of which escalated into violence, and ultimately resulted in more than one hundred deaths.

While critics of the cartoons described them as Islamophobic or racist, and argued that they were blasphemous to the people of the Muslim faith, supporters said that the cartoons illustrated an important issue in a period of Islamic terrorism; their publication was a legitimate exercise of the right of free speech. A Pew Global Attitudes survey released on 22 June 2006, a year after the riots over the Prophet's cartoon, found that many in the West see Muslims as fanatical, violent, and lacking in tolerance, while Muslims in the Middle East and Asia generally see Westerners as selfish, immoral and greedy. The survey, conducted in thirteen countries including the United States, offers hope with respect to Muslim support for terrorism. In Jordan, Pakistan and Indonesia, there have been substantial declines in the per centage of people saying that suicide bombings and other forms of violence against civilian targets can be justified to defend Islam against its enemies.

While fanatic and terrorist leaders, who present themselves as the true voice of Islam, lose no occasion to address the Western population with their threats, no moderate Islamic voice is available to talk about the true message of Islam and its prophet.

18

Muhammad's Islam

Now that we have seen the life of the Prophet of Islam, we can try to understand what kind of a religion he gave his people, and see whether Muhammad's religion was a faith or a political movement.

As the last verse of the Qur'an, which was delivered a few months before Muhammad's death (5:3), confirms that Islam has been completed by that time, nothing that was produced after that date could be regarded as part of the Islamic religion. While Muslim scholars have always had the right to explain and interpret the Qur'an and Sunna, they had no right to change the clear understanding of the original text, either by making new additions or by excluding any of its obligations. The Qur'an itself includes many statements which forbid any change of its words: 'There is none that can alter the Words (and Decrees) of Allah' (6:34); while a saying attributed to the Prophet confirms the same meaning: 'Know that every renewal in God's religion is a heresy, and every heresy is a deviation from what is right, and every deviation is in Hell.'

This means that, contrary to the attempts by some modern groups of political Islam to regard Christians and Jews as unbelievers, both the Qur'an and *sunna*, regard them as People of the Book, who share with Muslims the belief in the unity of God. Moreover, the Qur'an speaks of Christians as being the nearest people in love to Muslims: 'those who say: "We are Christians"; because amongst these are men devoted to learning and men who have renounced the world, and they are not arrogant.' (5:82)

What is Islam?

The Qur'an, in many of its verses, makes it clear that the Prophet's message was founded on belief and worship for the one God, abiding by good ethics and wise speech, and following the correct direction established on wisdom and good advice. Whoever studies these verses of the Qur'an will find that it orders the Prophet to adhere in his mission to truth, good speech, proper instruction and harmless behaviour: 'O Prophet! We have sent you as a Witness, a Bearer of Glad Tidings, and a Warner, And as one who invites to Allah's (Grace) by His leave, and as a Lamp spreading Light.' (33:45–6)

When we examine the new faith breached by Muhammad to the Arabs in the early seventh century AD, we find that Islam, like any other religion, is built on two main elements: belief and worship. Muslims believe in one God who has no image, the resurrection of the dead at the Day of Judgement, and they also believe that Muhammad is the Prophet of God and that the Qur'an contains the revealed word of Allah. Islam is framed within what is known as the five pillars, namely:

The Shahadah, or testimony, that God is absolutely One.
The five daily prayers, at morning, noon, afternoon, sunset and evening.
The fast of Ramadan, for one lunar month.
The Zakat, the payment of 2.5 per cent of each Muslim's yearly profit.
The pilgrimage to Mecca, once in a lifetime for those who can afford it.

Islamic sources

Islamic doctrine, law, and thinking in general are based upon two main sources: the Qur'an and the Sunnah (traditions). The Qur'an is regarded as the Word of God delivered to Muhammad by the angel Gabriel. Divided into 114 chapters, it is the fundamental source of Islamic teaching. While the chapters revealed at Mecca during the earliest part of Muhammad's career are concerned mostly with ethical and spiritual teachings as well as the Day of Judgment, those revealed later at Medina are concerned for the most part with social legislation and moral principals.

Sunnah means the example of the Prophet; i.e. his words and deeds as later recorded in compilations known as *Hadith*, which is revered and received as a major source of religious law, second only to the authority of the Qur'an. However, while the Qur'an was completed before Muhammad's death and compiled about ten years later, the development of *Hadith* took place some time after the death of the Prophet, during the first three centuries of the Islamic state. Six of the written documents, compiled in the ninth century, came to be regarded as especially authoritative by the Sunnis, the largest group in Islam, while the Shi'ites, the second largest group, has its own collection of *Hadith*.

Thus we can see that the religion of Islam which the Prophet has preached was a faith and belief, not a political program. The Islamic mission preached by Muhammad was neither related to the reorganisation of society and redistribution of wealth, nor with changing the government of Mecca. In fact when Muhammad became like a thorn in Meccan's back with his new religion, they asked him to be their ruler and he refused.

Muhammad and violence

The biography of Muhammad is the story of a man who became an orphan even before his birth, and suffered great injustice and oppression during his life. However, when ridiculed or physically harmed by his opponents, Muhammad never tried to respond in the same way, but acted with tolerance and patience. He even decided to leave his home at Mecca and migrated to Medina to escape an assassination attempt by the Quraysh, and although he fought many tribal wars after he moved to Medina, Muhammad never used force to persuade people to join his religion.

In *Al-Sira Al- Nabawiya*, (the Biography of the Prophet) Ibn Hisham, who died in Egypt about two centuries after Muhammad's mission, states that when Muhammad first addressed his people with the message of Islam, they rejected him and united in their enmity to him. However, Abu Talib, his uncle, protected him and refused to deliver him to them. Some of the Quraysh nobles went to Abu Talib and told him: 'Your nephew has insulted our gods and criticised our religion; either you restrain him or let us deal with him.'

Abu Talib did not agree to their request, but sent them back after having spoken nicely to them. The Quraysh then thought to spread rumours against the Prophet, giving him a bad name, so that people would get away from him. Ibn Hisham states that Muhammad then prayed to God, saying: 'O God, to you I complain about my weakness, my little power, people's contempt for me. O, you who are the most Merciful, the Lord of the oppressed.' Here, Muhammad did not ask for weapons to fight his enemies, but mercy to help him bear their abuse so that he could continue his mission.

Neither when he was weak in Mecca nor later when he became strong and able to enter the Arabs' holy city in victory did Muhammad use threats or weapons to force people into his faith; rather he tried to convince them, using spiritual and logical methods.

Jewish and Christian influence

Islam has two main elements of belief; the realisation of the unity of God the Creator who has no image, in which it agrees with the teaching of Moses and the Jewish religion, and the belief in eternal spiritual life, the resurrection of the dead and the last judgment, in which it agrees with the Christian message. It is a Judeo-Christian religion, combining both the monotheistic teaching of Moses and the Christian belief of the resurrection. As he regarded his message as a confirmation of earlier prophets, Muhammad never claimed that he was preaching a new religion. On the contrary, he stressed from the start that Islam was the very same Hanif faith of Abraham, the great ancestor of both the Israelites and the Ishmaelites. He accepted all the earlier prophets of the Old Testament, and confessed that Jesus was the Messiah, born of the Virgin Mary who was resin from the dead.

Accordingly, we can expect to find many similarities and agreements between Muhammad's teaching and the teaching of both the Old and New testaments. The Qur'an itself accepts the Torah and the Gospel as distinctly revealed scriptures and declares that there is an inner correspondence between Islam and both Judaism and Christianity. Western scholars, however, have relied on these similarities to dismiss Muhammad's claim for prophecy and regard him as an impostor. In the nineteenth century, some biblical scholars attempted to examine the Qur'an by applying the same new method they used for biblical criticism. These methods treated the holy texts in the same way as they treat ordinary literary work, trying to know the time and place a text originated and by whom. They used this method to study textual, compositional, and historical questions surrounding the Qur'an in order to lay the groundwork for meaningful interpretation of the holy book of Islam. In this way they focused their efforts on the question of the source of the Qur'an and Islam, and were mainly interested in the investigation of foreign influences on Muhammad.

It was then that the common ground between the Bible and the Qur'an became obvious; the stories of creation and the flood, Abraham as the great ancestor of the prophets, the accounts of Joseph, Moses and Jesus; all this material was found in both sources. However, while Muslim scholars regarded these similarities as coming from the same inspired source, biblical scholars saw it as evidence of the biblical influence on Islam. They regarded his main achievement as borrowing some Jewish and Christian teaching which, according to them, he mixed with ancient Arabian traditions to formulate his religion. It was believed that researching Islam's dependence on the older revealed religions would lead to a better understanding of Islam itself, and from the start, Islam was closely tied to Judaism and Christianity. In 1936, Tor Andrae, a German scholar, defined the task of the scholarly study of Muhammad as an attempt to understand how he forged numerous elements of the most varied sort into one living whole. 'That the fundamental ideas of Islam were borrowed from the Biblical religions is a fact which requires no further discussion.' (Tor Andare, *Mohammed*, translated from German by Theophil Menzel, London, 1936, p. 11) However, while Jewish scholars often came to the conclusion that Islam was to be viewed as an offshoot of Judaism, Christian scholars insisted on its Christian origins.

Jewish Influence

In 1833 Abraham Geiger, a German Jewish Rabbi who led the foundation for Reform Judaism, where he sought to remove all nationalistic elements (particularly the 'Chosen People' doctrine) from Judaism, expressed his view that Islam owed a tremendous debt to Hebraic writings and traditions. (Abraham Geiger, *Was hat Mohammed aus dem Judenthume aufgenommen*? Bonn, 1933, translated into English by F. M. Young under the name *Judaism and Islam,* Madras, 1898) This line of thought was followed by a number of scholars who wrote on the subject of Jewish influence on the Qur'an, supporting Geiger's view:

> Unquestionably the first impression gained by a reader of the Koran is that Muhammad had received the material of his new faith and practice mainly from the Jews of the Hijaz. On almost every page are encountered either episodes of Hebrew history, or familiar Jewish legends, or details of rabbinical law or usage, or arguments which say in effect that Islam is the faith of Abraham and Moses.
>
> [Charles C. Torrey, *The Jewish Foundation of Islam*, Jewish Institute of Religion Press, New York, 1933, p. 2]

These scholars noted that, like the Jew, the Muslim affirms the unity of God. God is one, eternal, merciful, compassionate, beneficent, almighty, all-knowing, just, loving and forgiving. The practice of reading the Qur'an at Friday Assemblies and other religious holidays follows the Jewish pattern. Muhammad chose Friday to take the place of the Jewish Sabbath and the Christian Sunday. The Qur'anic stories of the Creation, life in Paradise, the question as to whether earth or heavens came first, the objection of the angels to the creation of man, Adam's remarkable wisdom, Satan's rejection of Adam, Adam and Eve in the garden of Eden, and Adam's universal lesson for repentance all stem from biblical and midrashic elements. The stories about Israel's covenant with God; the travails in Egypt; the miracles at the Red Sea; the making of the golden calf after Moses went up the mountain; the Israelites' request to see God manifestly in order to believe in Him; the restoration of the stricken dead to life; the pillar of cloud; the manna and the quails; Moses' smiting of the rock; the objection to the taste of the manna; the giving of the Torah by 'raising the mountain'; the breakers of the Sabbath; the red heifer: all these stories in the Qur'an are traceable to Jewish origins. Likewise, the concepts of ethical monotheism, the unity of God, prayer, consideration for the underprivileged, reverence for parents, fasting, penitence, belief in angels, the stories about Abraham, the Patriarchs, Samuel, Saul, David, Solomon, the injunction of a pilgrimage to Mecca, waging war against the enemy, the status of women, and the position of prophets all have their antecedents in Jewish tradition.

Realising the similarities between Jewish and Muslim beliefs in many essential points, these scholars of oriental studies asserted that this was due to Jewish influence on Muhammad. They recognised that the canonical obligations or the pillars of Islam as well as a great number of names or narratives in the Qur'an have their biblical and Aggadic counterparts. Adam, Noah, Abraham are mentioned seventy times each; Ishmael, Lot, Joseph, Saul, David, Solomon, Elijah, Job and Jonah figure prominently. Moses' name occurs in thirty-four Suras. The story of the Creation and the Fall of Adam is cited five times and the Flood and Sodom eight times. (Abraham I. Katsh, *Judaism in Islam*, New York, 1954, p. xix)

Christian influence

Following Geiger's assertion of Jewish influence which held the field for many years, there was a reaction later in the nineteenth century in favour of Christianity as the main source of Muhammad's inspiration. To this, the great influence of Julius Wellhausen, the noted German biblical scholar and orientalist, gave an impetus which has lasted ever since. In his *Reste arabischen Heidentums* (1887),

Wellhausen, who had studied ancient Arabic paganism, pre-Islamic Medina, and Muhammad's constitution of Medina, treated briefly the origin of Islam, which he held to be largely Christian. Many others followed Wellhausen in the same track, asserting that the influence of Christianity on Islam was more potent than that of Judaism: 'Adolf von Harnack, famous historian of the early church, is known to have called Islam a Christian sect.' (Heribert Busse, *Islam, Judaism, and Christianity*, Markus Wiener, 1999, p. 3)

What persuaded many scholars to agree with Wellhausen was the close similarity between Islam and Christianity regarding the End of Days:

> It is what we may call, generally, apocalyptic material, the description of the End of the World, the Judgement Day, the Pains of Hell for the wicked, and the Joys of Heaven for the believers. All this material is directly borrowed. In fact, so far as the descriptions of the End of the World are concerned, almost every detail of them can be paralleled in well-known books of Apocalyptic.
>
> [Richard Bell, *The Origin of Islam*, Frank Cass, 1968, pp. 103–4]

According to Christian eschatology, the Last Judgment or Day of the Lord is the simultaneous judgment of every human, after the resurrection of the dead, by Jesus Christ before the Great White Throne to either eternal life or oblivion in the lake of fire at the end of time. The doctrine and iconographic features of a 'Last Judgment' appear most directly in The Sheep and the Goats section of the Book of Matthew:

> When the Son of man shall come in his glory, and all the holy angels with him, then shall he sit upon the throne of his glory: And before him shall be gathered all nations: and he shall separate them one from another, as a shepherd divideth his sheep from the goats: And he shall set the sheep on his right hand, but the goats on the left. Then shall the King say unto them on his right hand, Come, ye blessed of my Father, inherit

> the kingdom prepared for you from the foundation of the world . . . Then shall he say also unto them on the left hand, Depart from me, ye cursed, into everlasting fire, prepared for the devil and his angels . . . And these shall go away into everlasting punishment: but the righteous into life eternal.
>
> [Matthew, 25:31–34, 41, 46]

Resurrection

The belief in the resurrection of the body is usually associated with Christianity, because of the doctrine of the Resurrection of Christ. The resurrection of Christ, a central doctrine of Christianity, is based on the belief that Jesus Christ was raised from the dead on the third day after his Crucifixion and that through his conquering of death all believers will subsequently share in his victory over death. Islam also teaches a doctrine of the resurrection, where at Doomsday all men will die and then be raised from the dead. Then, each person will be judged according to the record of his life that is kept in two books, one listing the good deeds, the other the evil. After the Judgment the wrongdoers will be placed in hell and the faithful will go to paradise. The Qur'an speaks of 'Yom Al Kiyamah', the Day of Resurrection, which is also the Day of Judgment, something like a Final Judgment or Day of Reckoning. Islam teaches the bodily resurrection of the dead, the fulfilment of a divine plan for creation, and the immortality of the human soul; the righteous are rewarded with the pleasures of *Jannah* (Heaven), while the unrighteous are punished in *Jahannam* (Hell).

19

The Caliphate

Nation and State

The popular notion that Islam is a religion and a state represents some misunderstanding, due to the fact that those rulers who established the Islamic state regarded themselves as successors of the Prophet. When the Islamic state expanded outside the Arabian Peninsula, reaching the Chinese borders in East Asia, and Spain in Western Europe, those nations who were conquered by the Islamic state and converted to Islam gave their loyalty to a Caliph, who, as well as being emperor, was regarded as the Prophet's successor. In this situation, it was natural for the new converts to regard Islam as both a religion and a state. It was the nature of a Caliph's dual position as a ruler and religious leader that created confusion in understanding the nature of Islam and whether it was a faith or a political movement.

Although during the last years of his life, Muhammad was able to unite the tribes of Arabia into a single community, the Prophet himself did not form a ruling government or a political state; rather, he formed the Islamic nation (*umma*).

> During the last two years of his life, the Prophet had received the submission of most of the tribes of Arabia. This did not, of course, mean that the peninsula constituted a political unity, governed and administered from Medina. Submission involved two actions only: a nominal adherence to the Muslim religion and the payment of an annual tax. When Muhammad was alive, there was no government and no paid army. What revenue came into Medina was immediately distributed to the poor.
>
> [John Glubb, *A Short History of the Arab Peoples*, p. 42]

There is a difference between a nation and a s
represents a large group of people with strong bo
who share common history, culture, language or et
state is a politically organised body of people unde
government. A state has a 'monopoly on the legitimate use o physical force within a given territory', which may include the armed forces, civil service or state bureaucracy, courts, and the police. However, up to the last day of his life, the Prophet Muhammad did not form a ruling government for the Muslim community; neither did he speak of one. He had no bureaucracy, no organised army, and no constitution.

Succession

Immediately it became known in Medina that Muhammad had died, even before his body was prepared for burial, dispute broke out about the future of the Muslim community he had established. While the Helpers (*Ansar*) of Medina wanted to separate themselves from those emigrants who had come with Muhammad from Mecca, the Meccan companions of the Prophet wanted to keep the unity of the Bedouin tribes under their leadership, by appointing a successor for the dead Prophet.

For hundreds of years before Islam, the Arabian Peninsula lived in a state of continuous warfare between the different Bedouin tribes. Except for some settlements around the oases, such as Medina and Mecca in western Arabia, the greater part of the peninsula consisted of deserts inhabited by nomadic tribes, breeders of camels, sheep and goats. When Muhammad introduced his new religion of Islam to those tribes in the early seventh century AD, he was able to unite the different tribes behind the banner of Islam. During the last two years of his life, following his victory over Mecca in January 630, most of the Arab tribes, except those on the frontiers of Syria and Iraq in the north, sent deputations to Medina seeking alliance with the Prophet. In return Muhammad demanded acceptance of Islam, which included, acknowledgment of his own prophethood, and payment of the 'alms' or *zakat*, to be distributed to the poor. During these years, the lives of the Arabs were transformed, as they became one nation under one flag of one God: Allah.

When Muhammad died at Medina in 632, it looked as if the Islamic tribal coalition he had established was going to break up. However Muhammad did not establish a political unity which he governed and administered from Medina, and the Arabs were still living under the same old tribal rules. Their submission was to Muhammad personally, not as a ruler, but as a Prophet, which is why as soon as the tribes of the peninsula heard of his death, most of them stopped paying the (*zakat*) alms tax, which they used to pay him.

When the Prophet died at Medina, it looked as if that was the end of the Islamic tribal coalition which he had established in the Arabian Peninsula. The Ansar (Helpers) of Medina, who supported Muhammad and fought for him against his own Meccan people, decided to form their own community and chose one of them to be their leader. So, while Muhammad's body was still laid on his bed, locked in Ayesha's apartment at the same spot where he died, they met in the roofed passage (portico) of Banu Sa'ida and decided to separate themselves from the Emigrants (Al-Muhajirun) and choose one of their own as a leader. However, as they were about to vote for Sa'd ibn Ubadah (the chief of the Khazraj, who was a prominent companion of the Prophet) to be their leader, the Emigrants of Quraysh found out about their movement.

The Emigrants gathered around Abu Bakr, Muhammad's close friend and father-in-law, whom they regarded as their leader. When Abu Bakr was informed about the Helper's decision to choose one of them as their leader, Umar advised Abu Bakr to go to the Ansar to see what they were doing. Umar later described what happened in a Friday speech:

> After the death of the Prophet we were informed that the Ansar did not gather with us and gathered in the shed of Bani Sa'da. (At the same time) Ali and Zubair and whoever was with them, did not come with us, while the . . . I said to Abu Bakr, 'Let's go to these Ansari brothers of ours.' So we set out seeking them . . . we reached them at the shed of Bani Sa'da. Behold! There was a

man sitting amongst them and wrapped in something. I asked, 'Who is that man?' They said, 'He is Sa'd bin 'Ubada.' I asked, 'What is wrong with him?' They said, 'He is sick . . . ' we sat for a while, (then) the Ansar's speaker said, ' . . . we are Allah's Ansar (helpers) and the majority of the Muslim army, while you, the emigrants, are a small group . . . '

When the speaker had finished . . . I (Umar) wanted to speak, (but) Abu Bakr said, 'Wait a while.' . . . So Abu Bakr himself gave a speech, and he was wiser and more patient than I . . . he said, 'O Ansar! You deserve all the qualities that you have attributed to yourselves, but this question (of leadership) is only for the Quraysh as they are the best of the Arabs as regards descent and home, and I am pleased to suggest that you choose either of these two men, so take the oath of allegiance to either of them as you wish.' And then Abu Bakr held my hand and Abu Ubada bin Abdullah's hand . . . then one of the Ansar said, 'There should be one prince from us and one from you.'

[Al-Bukhari on the authority of Ibn Abas in Kitab Al-Hudood (see *Fath Al-Bari* vol. 12)]

This offer was followed by a hot dispute among the gathering, whose voices rose high. Then Umar, who feared that this dispute could result in disagreement, decided to put an end to the argument. Umar realised that in order to keep the Islamic nation united, someone must succeed Muhammad as the new head of the Islamic community. With some of his followers, he jumped over the sick Sa'd ibn Ubadah, the Ansar's choice for a leader, and he died instantly. At the same time Umar announced his pledge of allegiance for Abu Bakr to be the leader, and was followed by the rest of the emigrants and the Ansar followed afterwards. One of the Ansar said to Umar: 'you have killed Sa'd ibn Ubadah', and Umar replied: 'It was God that killed him.' (Ibn Hisham, *Sira*, p. 176)

After lengthy arguments, Umar succeeded in winning general acceptance for Abu Bakr, Muhammad's close friend and father-in-law, as Khalifat rasul-Allah, or successor of God's Apostle. Thus, thanks to Umar history has changed its course and the nation of

Islam became a state, known as the Caliphate, which was formed in AD 632 in Medina before it was enlarged when the Arabs subjected the countries of the Near and Middle East and North Africa to their rule. During it's nearly thirteen centuries until it was dissolved by Kemal Ataturk in 1924, the caliphate remained a potent symbol of Muslim unity.

Although during his life, Muhammad appointed neither a deputy nor a successor, the Caliph was not just a ruler; he was both the guardian of faith as well as the community. The caliph was regarded both as Islam's religious leader, the 'Successor of the Prophet', as well as the political head of the emerging Islamic state. As they were close companions of Muhammad, the first four Caliphs: Abu Bakr, Umar, Uthman and Ali are commonly known by Sunnis as the *Khulafa-a-Rashideen* (rightly guided successors).

Wars of Apostasy

Having chosen Abu Bakr as Muhammad's successor, the companions went out of their meeting to prepare his body for burial, in the middle of the following night. Nevertheless, most of the Arabian tribes refused to be ruled by a central government, and refused to pay the *zakat* to Abu Bakr. With Umar's backing, the new Caliph decided to go to war against those rebellious tribes in order to force them to pay the *zakat*, now regarded as a government tax, and accept his authority as their ruler. These wars, which became known as the 'Wars of Apostasy', lasted for the whole of Abu Bakr's short rule of less than three years (632–4). Abu Bakr employed Khalid ibn Walid, a former pagan military leader, to subdue the rebellious tribes. Later Muslim writers described this rebellious movement as the *Ridda*, giving the term the specific sense of 'apostasy' from Islam. However, since they never abandoned Islam or thought of restoring paganism, the *Ridda* should not really be regarded as a religious apostasy, but instead a political rebellion. The *Ridda* wars were in fact a process of subjection of Arabian tribes to form a political unity under the central rule of Abu Bakr, in Medina. As the first Caliph spent his three years rule trying to impose a central government on the Arab tribes, it was left to the second Caliph, Umar ibn al Khattab (634–44), to establish the government and the army.

Zakat

Zakat, the alms-tax, is one of the five principal obligations of Islam. When the Prophet introduced it early while he was still in Mecca, zakat simply meant alms giving, and the practice was quite unregulated. The Qur'an and Tradition describe as recipients of the *zakat* certain categories of people; such as parents, relatives, orphans, poor, travellers, beggars and slaves. In Medina, conditions influenced the nature of the zakat; the poor believers who migrated from Mecca had to be supported by charity from the Ansar. On the other hand, Muhammad was now able to introduce some kind of organisation for the reception and distribution of *zakat*, which was used to support the needy in the Muslim community. Later, when Islam has spread among the Arabs, the collectors had to receive the *zakat* of the Bedouin tribes who had adopted Islam, the amount of which was usually fixed definitely in the agreements made with the Prophet. However, although it was preferable to hand the *zakat* to the Muslim authorities for regulated distribution, it was also permitted to hand it direct to those persons who had claims to it.

After Muhammad's death many Bedouin tribes refused to continue paying *zakat*, as they considered their agreements cancelled by the death of the Prophet. In his attempt to turn *zakat* into a permanent state tax, Abu Bakr established a state treasury which contributed greatly to the expansion of Muslim power. While *zakat* in the time of the Prophet was regarded as a charity for the poor and needy of the Muslim society, Abu Bakr transformed it into a political obligation. Later, when the Islamic state had expanded outside Arabia and the treasury was receiving vast amounts of money from foreign tribute, the Muslims in Arabia were no longer forced to pay *zakat* to the government. This situation lasted until the present time, as *zakat* has returned to its original character, being a charity for the poor and the needy.

Shari'a

When the Muslim community developed into an organised state and an empire, from the time of Umar the second Caliph, it needed to regulate its actions according to Islamic law. Relying on Qur'anic teaching and Muhammad's traditions, Muslim scholars produced different views and interpretations of what they regarded to be the right Islamic law. Where they were adopted by a ruler or a judge, these interpretations became regarded as part of Islamic law known as the Shari'a. Although it is a man made law, the Shari'a has been regarded as a divinely ordained path of conduct that guides the Muslim towards a practical expression of his religious conviction in this world, and the goal of divine favour in the world to come.

20

History of the Qur'an

The Qur'an is the central religious verbal text of Islam, and Muslims believe it to be the book of divine guidance and direction for mankind, the final revelation of God. The word Qur'an literally means 'the recitation', and Islam holds that the Qur'an was revealed verbally from God to Muhammad through the angel Gabriel, over a period of approximately twenty-three years, beginning in 610, when he was forty, and concluding in 632, the year of his death. The Prophet recited the verses of the Qur'an to his companions, who memorised it by heart, while some of them put it down in writing. According to Muslim historians, the Qur'an was memorised, recited and written down by the Prophet's companions after every revelation. While Moses is said to have divided the waters of the sea and Jesus was raised from the dead, Muslims regard the Qur'an as the main miracle of Muhammad, proof of his prophet hood. According to the Qur'an, Muhammad was an *ummi*, which is interpreted by some as being 'illiterate' who can't read or write, while others take it to mean a 'gentile', and not a descendant of the Israelites.

However, when Muhammad died in 632, the Qur'anic verses had not yet been gathered into a single book; they were recorded only on palm leaves and flat stones and in the hearts of men. Muslim tradition agrees that the Qur'an was memorised by some companions before it was established textually into a single book form shortly after Muhammad's death by order of the first Caliph Abu Bakr. After seventy reciters were killed in the Battle of Yamama, the Caliph decided to collect the different chapters and verses into one volume. Thus, a group of reciters collected the chapters and verses and produced several handwritten copies of the complete book.

This first text was entrusted to Hafsa, Muhammad's widow and Umar's daughter, after the second Caliph Umar passed away.

In the early decades of the Arab conquests, many members of Muhammad's coterie were killed; with them died valuable knowledge of the Qur'anic revelations. Muslims at the edges of the empire began arguing over what was Qur'anic scripture and what was not. It was then that Caliph Uthman (644–56), the third Islamic ruler, started noticing differences in the dialect of the Qur'an; he requested Hafsa to allow him to use the Qur'an text in her possession to be set as the standard Classical Arabic. In about 650, Uthman convened an editorial committee that gathered the various pieces of scripture which had been memorised or written down by Muhammad's companions. Five reciters from amongst the companions produced a unique text from the first volume which had been prepared on the orders of Abu Bakr and which was kept with Hafsa daughter of Umar. The copies already in the hands of Muslims in other areas were collected and sent to Medina where, on the Caliph's orders, they were destroyed by burning or boiling. This remains the authoritative text of the Qur'an to this day.

The Qur'an represents the same monotheistic beliefs and stories as the Bible. God, who has created the world and its creatures, is the supreme ruler. He is the all-powerful, all-knowing, and all-merciful Being, who sends messages and laws through prophets to help guide human existence. At some time in the future, known only to him, God will bring about the end of the world and the Day of Judgment. Adam, the first man, is expelled from Paradise for eating from the forbidden tree, and Noah builds an ark to save a select few from a flood brought on by the wrath of God. Abraham, the great ancestor of both Israelites and Arabs, prepares himself to sacrifice his son at God's bidding, while Moses leads the Israelites out of Egypt and receives a revelation on Mount Sinai. Jesus, born of the Virgin Mary, is the Messiah who works miracles, has disciples, and rises to heaven after his death.

During the next few centuries, while Islam spread with the conquests of the empire, a vast body of exegetical and historical literature evolved to explain the Qur'an and the history of Islam, the most important elements of which are *hadith*, or the collected sayings and deeds of the Muhammad; *sunna*, which is the body of Islamic social and legal custom; *sira*, the biographies of the Prophet; and *tafsir*, or Koranic commentary and explication. It is from these traditional sources, compiled in written form mostly from the mid-eighth to the mid-tenth century, that all accounts of the revelation of the Qur'an and the early years of Islam have been derived.

About the same length as the New Testament, the text of the Qur'an consists of 114 chapters of varying lengths, each known as a *sura*. Chapters are classed as Meccan or Medina, depending on where the verses were revealed. Chapter titles are derived from a name or quality discussed in the text, or from the first letters or words of the *sura*. The longer chapters appear earlier in the Qur'an, while the shorter ones appear later, thus the chapter arrangement is not related to the sequence of revelation. Each *sura*, except the ninth, starts with the *Basmala*, an Arabic phrase meaning 'In the name of God, Most Gracious, Most Merciful'. There are, however, still 114 occurrences of the basmala in the Qur'an, due to its presence in verse 27:30 as the opening of Solomon's letter to the Queen of Sheba.

The issue of whether the Qur'an is eternal or created was one of the crucial controversies among early Muslim theologians. A major theological debate arose within Islam in the late-eighth century, pitting those who believed in the Qur'an as the 'uncreated' and eternal Word of God, against those who believed it to be created in time, in the same way as anything that is not God himself. Under the Abbasid Caliph al-Ma'mun (813–33), the view that it was uncreated became orthodox doctrine. It was supported by several schools of thought, including an influential one known as Mu'tazilah that developed a complex theology based partly on a metaphorical rather than simply literal understanding of the Qur'an.

By the end of the tenth century, the influence of the Mu'tazili school had waned for complicated political reasons, and the official doctrine had become that of i'jaz, or the 'inimitability' of the Qur'an. This is why the Qur'an has traditionally not been translated for non-Arabic-speaking Muslims. Instead it has been read and recited in the original by Muslims worldwide, the majority of whom do not speak Arabic. When it was translated later to other languages, these translations were considered to be nothing more than scriptural aids and paraphrases. The adoption of the doctrine of inimitability was a major turning point in Islamic history, and from the tenth century to this day the mainstream Muslim understanding of the Qur'an as the literal and uncreated Word of God has remained constant.

21

The Islamic Empire

When Muhammad died in 632, there were two major powers in control of the Middle East, the rival empires of Byzantium in the west and the Persian Sassanid in the east. While Byzantium controlled North Africa, Egypt, and the Levant, Persia controlled Mesopotamia. At the same time, Europe had lost its unifying political power following the collapse of the Western Roman Empire in 476 and was controlled by barbarian tribes for a period of about one thousand years, known as the Dark Ages. During this time the Roman Catholic Church was the only unifying force in Europe.

The Roman-Persian Wars had devastated the inhabitants of the two regions, making both empires unpopular amongst local tribes. Furthermore, most Christian Churches in the lands that would be conquered by Muslims (such as Nestorians, Monophysites, Jacobites and Copts) were under pressure from the Christian Orthodoxy, which deemed them heretics.

While this was going on, the Bedouin tribes of Arabia were united under the banner of Islam, and the emerging Arab state began to seek outward expansion. North of the Arabian Peninsula, the desert extended between the cultivated lands of Iraq in the east and the Levant in the west. The small Arabian Kingdom of Hira, on the Lower Euphrates, was allied with the Persian Empire, while the north-west Kingdom of Gassan, east of Damascus, was allied with the other great power of the period – Byzantium. These small Arabian buffer states of Hira and Gassan had already declined before the infant Arab state began to expand under Abu Bakr, the first Caliph, with a series of probing raids into Mesopotamia.

In March 633, one year after Muhammad's death, Khalid led his forces northwards up the Euphrates, defeating the local tribes as well as the Persian troops. In the spring of the same year, they occupied the town of Hira on the desert fringes of the southwestern Mesopotamia, whose population was Christian Arabs. In a period of nine months, Khalid was able to overrun the entire Iraqi desert up to the River Euphrates. The Arab forces he led consisted almost entirely of undisciplined tribesmen mounted on camels or horses.

In August 634, the Caliph Abu Bakr died in Medina and was succeeded by the strong-minded and autocratic Umar, who took the title of '*Amir al-Mu'mineen*' or commander of the believers. Umar, who finally established the Islamic state and organised its political and administrative bodies, sent a new commander to the Euphrates, Saad ibn Abi Waqqas. Around February 637, at Kadisiyya in southern Mesopotamia near the modern town of Nejef, a decisive battle was fought against the Persians, who had collected a great army under their commander-in-chief Rustem. After three days of fighting on the west bank of the Euphrates, Rustem was killed and the Arabs won the battle. They then drove on north to capture the Sassanid capital of Ctesiphon, south of Baghdad, and occupy all the lands of Mesopotamia. Over the next ten years the Arabs gradually reduced what remained of the Persian Sassanid Empire; its last emperor, Yazdajird, was killed in 651 as he fled. The Arab army then crossed the Oxus River in central Asia, and took Bukhara and Samarqand, while in the south they invaded the Sind in modern Pakistan.

At the time of the Arab conquests, Persia was Zoroastrian, while the Fertile Crescent and Egypt were largely Christian, with small Jewish communities. However, the ruling Byzantine authorities persecuted the Christian Nestorians and Monophysites in their lands in Syria, as they were regarded as heretics by the Byzantine Church. Monophystic teaching, which believes in a 'single nature' of Christ, had arisen in Egypt in the early fifth century, and was declared a heresy at the Fourth Ecumentic Council at Chalceden in 451. The struggle of the Byzantine government and the Greek Orthodox clergy, who believed in two natures of Christ, against the Monophysites degenerated at times into cruel bloody mass persecution. The inhabitants of Syria and Palestine, including Beni

Ghassan east of Damascus, were of the Christian Monophysite sect regarded as heretical by the Byzantine Orthodox Church.

During the rule of the second caliph, the Levant fell into Arab hands after a thousand years of Roman domination. When the Arabs turned to Syria, the Byzantine emperor, Heraclius, sent an army to meet the invaders. This army was decisively defeated by Khalid's forces in the crucial battle of Ajnadayn, in southern Palestine. Damascus fell in 636 and two years later Jerusalem surrendered to the Arabs. Patriarch Sophronius of Jerusalem insisted that he would only hand the city's keys to Caliph Umar in person. According to Arab historians, Umar made the journey to Jerusalem and gave his personal guarantee of the safety of the Christians, and their religious freedom. Having conquered the extensive and wealthy provinces of Syria, Palestine and Iraq, the Arab army marched from Caesarea on the Palestinian coast southwards towards Egypt. Amr ibn al-'As, the Arab general, arrived at the Roman fortress of Babilyon near modern Cairo with three thousand and six hundred men. Having destroyed the fortress, Amr then sailed up the Nile to Alexandria, which had over a million inhabitants at the time. The Arab army surrounded the walls of Alexandria for seven months before Emperor Heraclius was convinced to sign an agreement of surrender, and the Byzantine withdrawal was completed in September 642.

Soon after the fall of Alexandria, Amr decided to send his troops west, to occupy Barqa on the Libyan coast. The Byzantines had held a number of coastal fortresses in North Africa, while the interior of the country remained under the control of the local Berber tribes. Although it was easy for the Arabs to defeat the Byzantines in North Africa, it took them about a century to subdue the Berbers, who were then converted to Islam and became part of the Islamic empire. By the beginning of the eighth century, the last Byzantine cities in North Africa had been subdued, and a political fusion of Arabs and Berbers was forged. The great Arab/Berber cities of Kairouan (in Tunisia) and Fez (in Morocco) were founded, and the systematic settlement of the countryside began. By the early fifteenth century, the whole of North Africa, as far south as Lake Chad, and the area extending from Senegal on the Atlantic to

Somalia on the Indian Ocean were ruled by a network of Muslim governors.

In November 644, Caliph Umar was assassinated by a Persian slave while leading the prayers in Medina. He was followed by Uthman bin Affan, a member of the powerful Meccan Umayyad family. The third Caliph's reign, however, was confronted with many elements of internal disputes. Discontented tribesmen rose in revolt, and after eight years rule, Caliph Uthman too was murdered, while at prayer in his house at Medina. Ali ibn Abi Talib, the Prophet's cousin and husband of Fatima daughter of his first wife Khadija, was acclaimed as the fourth Caliph. Ali, however, was opposed by the powerful Umayyad family, who included Mu'awiya, the governor of Syria, and Ayesha, the Prophet's widow. Soon a military confrontation developed between the two sides and Ali, who had become master of Iraq, moving his capital from Medina to Kufa, went out to meet the rebels near the Iraqi-Syrian border. Just as he was on the verge of winning the battle of Siffeen, Ali gave away the victory. Mu'awiya's men refused to fight their Muslim fellows and fixed copies of the Qur'an to the points of their spears. Ali agreed to halt the fighting but during the arbitration which followed, representatives went to the Umayyads and some of the caliph's followers deserted him. They became known as the Kharijites (secessionists), and in January 661, one of them assassinated Caliph Ali in Kufa.

The Umayyad Dynasty

Following Ali's death, Mu'awiya, the Umayyad governor of Syria, proclaimed himself caliph in Jerusalem, forcing Ali's second son, Husayn, to give up his attempt to establish a rival caliphate in Iraq. Some Muslims, however, continued to believe in Ali and his descendants as the legitimate caliphs and to regard Mu'awiya and his Umayyad successors as usurpers. They became known as the *Shi'a* or 'partisans' of Ali, as opposed to the *Sunnis* or 'people of the *Sunna*' orthodox majority of Muslims. This led to a serious dissension within the Islamic nation, and ultimately to the great schism between Sunnis and Shi'as which has divided the Islamic world since. They built the town of Najaf in Iraq around Ali's supposed burial place, about 160 km south of Baghdad. Husayn was killed when he embarked on an abortive revolt against the Mu'awiya's son and successor in 680. He was buried north of Najaf at Karbala, which, together with Najaf, became the twin holy cities of the Shi'a, who are the majority in Iraq and represent about a tenth of Muslims worldwide.

The Umayyad Dynasty ruling from Damascus lasted for eighty-nine years from 661 to 750. During this time the Islamic expansion reached its peak, and a great empire was established. At first the fighting was done only by the Bedouin warriors who came out of Arabia, lured by the vast booty of the luxurious empires they conquered. Although Jews and Christians were reduced to the level of second-class citizens, they generally welcomed the Arabs because of the tyrannical rule of their previous masters. The new Muslim rulers treated the population of these lands in a better way. They regarded the adherents of the two heavenly religions, Judaism and Christianity as the 'People of the Book' (also known as *dhimmis)* who, under Islamic rule, enjoyed religious and personal toleration but not equality before the law. Their personal safety and property were guaranteed in return for a tribute imposed upon them. Since they paid most of the taxes, later mass conversions to Islam created a problem in reduced revenues. Under Islamic rule, the former subjects of Byzantium got their own well-established legal procedure, administered by trained members of the community.

The Arabs, however, were unable to conquer Byzantine Anatolia (Turkey today), despite persistent efforts, and they never succeeded in capturing Constantinople. In 670 an Arab fleet sailed through the Dardanelles and laid siege to Constantinople but failed to capture the Byzantine capital. Two years later another fleet captured the island of Rhodes and raided Sicily, which was finally taken from the Byzantines by the Arabs at the end of the ninth century. The Arab conquest of Sicily and southern Italy was eventually to provide one of the principal channels for the spread of Arab civilisation to Western Europe.

Andalusia

On the other hand, in April 711, Musa bin Nusair, the governor of North Africa, sent a force across the Straits of Gibraltar under a Berber freedman called Tariq ibn Ziyad. Although the unpopular Visigothic kingdom collapsed quickly, some of the cities held by the Gothic knights, such as Saville and Merida, continued to resist. By the end, in 714, the whole of Spain and Portugal except for a small independent state in the north-east had fallen into Muslim hands. Four years later, the Muslims broke through the eastern end of the Pyrenees into France and occupied Carcassonne and Narbonne. Within seven years, they had taken Nîmes in the south and their columns, moving up the Rhone valley, reached as far as Tours, halfway from the Pyrenees to Paris. In 741, however, civil war broke out between the Arabs and the Berbers in Spain, for which reason the invasion of France was abandoned.

Many Spaniards were converted to Islam and the converts (*muwallads*) formed an active element of the population. In the mean time, the majority of unconverted Christians enjoyed a high degree of tolerance and formed prosperous communities in the cities. The Muslims were more tolerant than the Goths, especially to the Jewish community, who had been persecuted for a long time; they therefore welcomed the Arabs and Berbers as liberators. The Muslims of Andalusia were far in advance of Western Europe in all forms of knowledge. From the end of the eighth century until about 1200, Muslim Spain was the most civilised and materially advanced part of Western Europe. Science and art were fostered, and Philosophy, medicine and mathematics were studied side by side with commerce and industry. At that time, Cordoba, with its seventy libraries and nine hundred public baths, was the most splendid city in Europe.

At the same time, while the Umayyad Dynasty flourished in Syria, various elements of discontent and division were brewing into a revolutionary movement based in Khorasan in eastern Persia. This movement rapidly advanced westwards, overthrowing the Umayyad ruler in 750. It then established the Dynasty of the Abbasids, who took their name from al-Abbas, one of the Prophet's uncles. This was the beginning of the golden age of the Abbasid caliphate, which moved the capital from Damascus to Baghdad, on the west bank of the river Tigris. Almost all members of the Umayyad family were massacred in Syria by order of the new Abbasid caliph.

However, one of the Umayyad princes, Abdul Rahman, managed to escape to Spain in 755. There, he was able to establish a strong centralised government based upon an imperial guard of Berbers and European slaves. It was under him and his successors – Abd al-Rahman II (822–52) and Abd al-Rahman III (912–61) – that the culture of Moorish Spain reached its zenith. The Abbasid Empire, which depended on Persian supporters, was more cosmopolitan and more sophisticated than that of the Umayyads. The first member of the Abbasid family to be proclaimed Caliph was Abu al-Abbas al-Saffah (750–4). He was followed by his brother, Abu Ja'far al-Mansur, who founded the city of Baghdad to be the new capital of the Islamic empire. The rule of the Abbasids reached its golden age at the time of Harun al-Rashid (775–809).

Throughout the Abbasids' rule, Muslims were very active militarily both on the land frontier with Byzantium and the vast arena of the Mediterranean. Nearly every year, the Arabs launched raids into Byzantine territory, which caused much economic damage to the frontier population. In February 782, Caliph Harun al-Rashid invaded Byzantine territory with twenty-five thousand men. Sweeping almost unopposed across Asia Minor, he camped on the shores of the Bosphorus, opposite Constantinople. Empress Irene, the widow of Constantine V, was compelled to accept a humiliating peace treaty, under the terms of which she promised to pay the Caliph an annual tribute of seventy thousand gold dinars. Irene was deposed by a revolution in Constantinople, however, and a member of the aristocracy mounted the throne with the title Nicephorus I in 802. Two years later Nicephorus refused to pay the tribute, demanding the repayment of all the tribute received from Constantinople. However, when Harun ordered an army to cross Asia Minor, Nicephorus was obliged to pay the tribute.

In the Mediterranean, Byzantium also suffered many defeats in the struggle with the Arabs, losing Crete in 825. This fertile island was seized by Muslim emigrants from Cordoba who had been driven out of Andalusia in 814, and all attempts by the Byzantines to recover Crete remained unsuccessful until 961. The Arabs of North Africa were also able to gain considerable success in the western Mediterranean. The conquest of Sicily by the ruler of Africa, Ziyadat Allah I of the Aghlabid dynasty, whose troops were able to occupy Palermo, Messina and most of the other cities on the island, left only Syracuse under Byzantine administration until the fall of the Amorian dynasty. From Sicily, the Arabs were able to cross into Italy and capture Taranto, which belonged to the Lombard Duke of Benevento, before they went on to take some points in Byzantine Calabria and Apulia.

During this period Baghdad, the capital of the Islamic Empire, reached the zenith of its glory under the Caliphs Harun al-Rashid and his son al-Mamun (813–33). Under Harun, the empire achieved its high noon of glory and wealth. Conversation and culture were considered arts: intellectual and theological discussions were among the recreations of the educated classes. The Caliph himself was well educated in religion, philosophy and literature, and his reign was marked by a high standard of intellectual activity. His son Mamun was devoted to books and to learned pursuits; his brilliant mind was interested in every form of intellectual activity. Poetry, philosophy, theology, astronomy, medicine and law: all occupied his time. His fourteen-year reign saw one of the most brilliant intellectual epochs in the history of the Islamic state. In Baghdad he opened an institution which he called the House of Wisdom, the principal object of which was to translate foreign works. In the first century of the Abbasid caliphate, most of the great works of Greek philosophy and science – Plato, Aristotle, Euclid and Hippocrates – were translated into Arabic.

The Abbasid Dynasty lasted about five hundred years before the Mongol general Hulagu, grandson of Genghis Khan, sacked Baghdad in 1258 and killed al-Musta'sim, the last caliph, who was sewn up in a sack and trampled to death under the feet of Mongol horses. Eight hundred thousand corpses were piled in the streets.

With the fall of the Abbasid dynasty in Baghdad, Arab rule of the Islamic Empire came to an end and the Turkomans became the new rulers of Islam, eventually establishing the Ottoman Empire which destroyed Byzantium, captured Constantinople and conquered eastern Europe.

22

Europe Hits Back

Crusaders

A hundred and sixty-three years before the fall of Abbasid Baghdad, Christian Europe launched its first counterattack against the Muslim Empire. Expeditions of European Crusaders marched east, charged with delivering the Holy Places in Palestine from Muslim hands. The idea of the crusade corresponded to a political conception that was realised in Christendom only from the eleventh to the fifteenth centuries, which supposes a union of all peoples and sovereigns under the direction of the popes. After pronouncing a solemn vow, each warrior received a cross, and was thenceforth considered a soldier of the Church.

A series of European crusades directed against Muslim control of Jerusalem and the Christian shrine of the Holy Sepulchre took place between the eleventh and thirteenth centuries. In 1095 Christendom launched the First Crusade, and for a century and a half Christian potentates attempted, with decreasing success, to establish Christian rule in Palestine and adjoining areas in the Near East. The capture of Jerusalem by the Crusaders in 1099 was a triumph for Christendom and a great loss for the Muslims. The newly established Crusader principalities from Antioch in northern Syria to Jerusalem in Palestine soon fitted into the game of Levantine politics, with cross-religious alliances in a pattern of rivalries between and among Muslim and Christian princes. However, the great Counter-Crusade by the Muslims did not begin until almost a century later. In 1182, in violation of an agreement between the Crusader king of Jerusalem and Saladin, the Muslim ruler of Egypt, the king attacked and looted Muslim caravans, including one made up of pilgrims bound for Mecca. It was these events that led directly to Saladin's proclamation of war against the Crusaders. Saladin was able to recapture Jerusalem from the Crusaders on 20 September 1187, which marked the beginning of the decline of the Crusaders in the east. On 18 May 1291, the Crusades came to an end after one hundred and ninety-four years of war.

Andalusia

A few years before the First Crusade left western Europe for the Levant, King Alfonso VI of Castile and Leon, based in the northwest of the Iberian Peninsula, captured Toledo in central Spain and obliged the petty Muslim states to pay him tribute. A deputation from Seville, Cordoba, Granada and Badajoz crossed to North Africa and solicited the aid of the Murabids, the Berber rulers of Maghrib. The Murabids crossed to Spain and on 23 October 1086, they routed Alfonso VI at Zallaka, (Sagrajas in Spanish history). They then removed most of the petty Arab dynasties and added Andalusia to their empire. Thus Andalusia fell under the control of North African rulers, first the Murabids and later the Muwahids, who were able to defend the country against the Christians.

However, 126 years later on 16 July 1212, Alfonso VIII raided Andalusia. The battle of Las Navas de Tolosa became the turning point in the reconquest of Spain. In this battle, the King of Castile was joined by Christian forces from Navarre, Aragon and Portugal. The Christians continued to press their advantage and in 1236 Cordoba, once the Umayyad capital, was captured. Valencia followed two years later. Eventually, with the fall of Granada in 1492, Muslim rule in the Iberian Peninsula came to an end when and Isabella succeeded in uniting Spain.

During the fifteenth century, the Christian kingdoms of Western Europe succeeded in driving the Muslims out of Spain, France, and Italy. However, after two centuries of fighting, the Crusaders in the east were forced to leave their positions in the Levant in Muslim hands. At the same time, following the fall of Arab rule in Baghdad, a new Islamic power appeared in the Middle East that posed more serious threats, not only to the Byzantine Empire, but also to Eastern Europe and the Balkan. In the fourteenth century the Ottoman Turks, who had settled in Anatolia about two centuries earlier, replaced the Seljuks as the major Islamic power. While the first Arab Muslim conquerors had been halted by the Byzantines at the Taurus Mountains, which marked the frontier between Islam and Christendom, the Turks succeeded in pushing the European barrier back, bringing Asia Minor into the world of Islam. The Ottomans resumed the Muslim attempt to conquer Europe, this time from the Balkans and the East. They first weakened Byzantium and then conquered much of the Balkans as well as North Africa. In May 1453, when the last Byzantine emperor fell while fighting on the walls of his city, the Turks captured Constantinople, which from then onwards became the capital of the Ottoman sultans under a new name – Istanbul.

23

The Rise and Fall of the Ottoman Empire

The Ottoman Empire, one of the most powerful states in the world during the fifteenth and sixteenth centuries, lasted for more than six hundred years and only came to an end after World War I in 1922. In the west it included most of southeastern Europe to the gates of Vienna, stretching over modern Hungary, Serbia, Bosnia, Romania, Greece, and Ukraine; while in the east it dominated Iraq, Syria, Palestine, Egypt, North Africa as far west as Algeria, and most of the Arabian Peninsula. The failure of the Ottomans to take Vienna in 1683, after their second besiege of the Austrian capital, marked the beginning of a long retreat. The defenders were able to build a major European coalition that was to bring destruction to the Ottoman Empire during the eighteenth century. The reign of Suleiman I, the Magnificent (1520–66) represented the peak of the Ottoman greatness and was followed by a gradual disintegration of the empire, whose boundaries continued to shrink. The Habsburgs set out to reconquer Hungary, Serbia, and the Balkans, while Venice hoped to regain its naval bases along the Adriatic Sea, and Russia wanted to extend its reach through the Bosphorus straits.

Egypt was one of the first Arab countries that managed to get out of Ottoman control, thanks to the French invasion. Modern history in the Middle East starts with the arrival in 1798 of the French expedition to Egypt under the command of Napoleon Bonaparte. The French forces landed at Abu Qir Bay near Alexandria on 1 July and took Alexandria the next day before marching south. They met little resistance and entered Cairo on 25 July. After the Ottoman viceroy and the Mamluks (foreign lords) ran away, Bonaparte decided to establish local councils of religious leaders, with the aim of communicating directly with the Egyptian population. Napoleon brought a commission of scholars and scientists with his military forces to investigate the history and condition of the country, as well as a printing machine to address the Egyptians in Arabic.

Bonaparte's success was, however, short lived. One month after his arrival to Egypt, the British Mediterranean fleet under Lord Nelson managed to destroy the French fleet at Abu Qir, virtually cutting his communication with France. In an attempt to strengthen his position in Egypt, Napoleon invaded Syria in February 1799, but he failed to take Acre, the centre of Ottoman governance on the Palestinian coast. Feeling trapped in foreign lands, Bonaparte decided to return to France and succeeded in slipping away past the British fleet on 22 August. As a result of the French expedition, Sultan Selim III was drawn into alliances with Great Britain. Napoleon's successors came under pressure from both British and Ottoman attacks and were forced to leave the country in September 1801.

Although the French occupation of Egypt lasted only three years, it had a great impact on the life and modern history of the country. After twelve centuries of Islamic rule, during which Egyptians had had no part in running their country, the Egyptian leaders had to deal directly with the new invader following the withdrawal of Ottoman and Mamluk protection. After the French withdrawal, the Ottomans re-established their power through a viceroy and an occupation army, in which the most effective fighting force was an Albanian contingent. The Albanians, however, installed their own leader as acting viceroy. When he was assassinated shortly afterward, the command of the Albanians passed to his lieutenant, Muhammad Ali, who was invested by the Egyptian leaders as viceroy during their revolt in May 1805. Faced with a popular unrest, Sultan Selim III was obliged to confirm Muhammad Ali in office.

Wahhabis

Soon after the eviction of the French from Egypt, the Ottomans were faced with a new conflict, this time in the Arabian Peninsula, where a movement of Islamic puritan revival known as Wahhabism appeared in Central Arabia. The leader of the movement, Muhammad ibn Abd al-Wahhab was a theologian from the Najd area, which was ruled by local sheikhs of the House of Saud. The Wahhabi movement was founded on the Hanbali school, the most literalist of all the four Sunni or orthodox schools of Islam, and on the fundamentalist teachings of Ibn Taymiya, the fourteenth-century religious leader. They were particularly opposed to Sufism (spiritual Islam), condemning not only its mysticism and tolerance but also what they saw as the pagan cults associated with it.

The Wahhabi religious cause was embraced by the Saudi rulers of Najd, who promoted it, and soon the religious campaign developed into a military campaign against the Ottomans. In a series of campaigns, the Wahhabis carried their rule, as well as their faith, to much of central and eastern Arabia and raided the lands of Syria and Iraq, which were under direct Ottoman administration. After sacking Karbala, the Shi'ite holly city in Iraq, they turned their attention to the Hijaz in west Arabia, and in 1804–6 occupied the holy cities of Mecca and Medina. The Ottoman Sultan Mahmud II called upon his Egyptian vassal in Egypt, Muhammad Ali, to suppress the Wahhabi rebellion. Muhammad Ali sent an expedition to Arabia, which between 1811 and 1813 expelled the Wahhabis from the Hejaz. In a further campaign (1816–18), Ibrahim Pasha, the viceroy's eldest son, defeated the Wahhabis in their homeland of Najd, sent the Saudi prince to be decapitated in Istanbul, and brought central Arabia within Egyptian control.

Muhammad Ali's Egypt

Seven years later, when an uprising began in the Peloponnese in southern Greece, the sultan again demanded Muhammad Ali's assistance. This time the Egyptian viceroy sent his troops to reinforce the Ottomans and was about to put down the revolt. However, the European powers intervened to destroy both the Egyptian and Ottoman fleets at Navarino in the southwestern Peloponnese on 20 October 1827; this forced the Ottomans to recognise Greek independence in 1832. Following the Greek war, the honeymoon between Istanbul and Cairo came to an end. Muhammad Ali, who was carrying through a radical program of modernisation, decided to take Egypt out of the Ottoman Empire. He even invaded Syria, defeating the Ottoman army near Konya in Anatolia (December 1832), and threatened the Ottoman capital at Istanbul. However, the European powers intervened for a second time, this time on the side of the Ottoman Sultan, and forced the Egyptian troops out of Syria. Nonetheless, they recognised Muhammad Ali as a hereditary ruler of Egypt in 1841.

Muhammad Ali's military exploits would not have been possible if not for the radical changes he introduced in the administration of Egypt itself. His military successes had been partly due to his employment of European officers, doctors and other officials, by which means he put Egypt on the path of modernisation. When his attempt to introduce Western methods of training to the army failed, he took the momentous step in 1823 of conscripting Egyptian peasants, for the first time under Islamic rule, for the rank and file of his new army. The viceroy gradually built a new administrative structure, including councils of officials, and administrative departments that had some resemblance to the ministries of European governments. These changes necessitated the training of officers and officials in the new European ways of working, which resulted in the creation of a range of educational institutions alongside the traditional Islamic schools. While the foundation work was done by expatriates, missions of Egyptian students were sent to Europe, especially to Paris.

Ottoman decline

After Suleiman's reign, when the Ottoman Empire had reached its greatest military power in the world, the nations of Europe cooperated to drive the Ottomans off their continent. By the succession of Mahmud II in 1808, the Ottoman situation appeared desperate, while the boundaries of the empire continued to shrink. The main reason behind the Ottoman decline and Europe's progress was the lack of modern education and technology. While the Ottoman Empire was still using handmade tools from the Middle Ages, Western Europe, following the Industrial Revolution in England in the eighteenth century, was witnessing a major technological development, relying on scientific discoveries and new invented machines. Very few of the innovations in technology that underlay Europe's prosperity made their way into the empire. The Ottoman situation appeared desperate, and decline set in. In 1878, the Ottomans were forced to give up Romania, Serbia, Montenegro, Bulgaria, Cyprus and other territories.

Under the Ottoman rule, following the fall of Islamic centres of education and culture in Baghdad and Andalusia, the Muslim world entered a new dark age. Education in the Empire was directed mainly towards religion and provided by Islamic groups. The Arabs of Spain had been far in advance of Western Europe in all forms of knowledge. The University of Cordoba was world famous and many Christians from Western Europe went there for their studies. Science and art were fostered side by side with commerce and industry. A series of Ottoman reforms promulgated during the mid-nineteenth century to produce specialists for the army failed to achieve any serious change either in the education system or the production methods, as culture, science, commerce and industry were contemptuously abandoned.

The fall of the empire

After about six hundred years, the Ottoman Empire collapsed at the end of World War I. The Ottoman entry into World War I on the side of the Germans resulted from an overly hasty calculation of likely advantage. Except for the interest of Russia in Istanbul and the Straits, no European power had genuinely vital interests in the Ottoman Empire. In 1918 the Ottoman sultanate was finally defeated and its capital, Constantinople, occupied. Its sovereign was taken captive and its Arab provinces divided between the victorious British and French Empires. In November 1922, the thirty-sixth and final Ottoman sultan, Mehmed VI Vahideddin, was overthrown. The declaration of the Turkish Republic, the first secular Islamic state, took place in 1923. The Sykes-Picot Agreement of 16 May 1916, the secret Anglo-French-Russian accord, and the mandate system, which was approved by the Allied Supreme Council on 20 April 1920 for the former Arab provinces of the Ottoman Empire, ushered in the next stage of the evolution of Arab nationalism. The agreement was a clear decision in principle to divide the Fertile Crescent into spheres of British and French influence.

The former Ottoman provinces of the Fertile Crescent were divided into three new entities, with new names and frontiers. Two of them, Iraq and Palestine, were under British Mandate; the third, under the name Syria, was given to the French. Later, the French subdivided their mandate into two, calling one part Lebanon and retaining the name Syria for the rest. In Palestine, the British created a division between the two banks of the Jordan. The eastern part was called Transjordan, later simply Jordan; the name Palestine was retained for the Western part. As the result of a determined struggle for independence waged under the leadership of the Ottoman wartime general Mustafa Kemal, later known as Ataturk, the Turks eventually succeeded in liberating their Anatolian homeland from Western domination.

24

People of the Book

'People of the Book' is a term used to designate non-Muslim adherents to faiths which have a book of prayer. The two faiths that are mentioned in the Qur'an as *people of the book* are Judaism and Christianity. They are cited as followers of the religions which, like Islam, do not worship idols. So there is a common agreement between Muslims and the People of the Book on the unity of God who has no image. Although '*Alkitab*' indicates one specific Book, this term is used for the followers of all the Bible prophets who appeared before Muhammad: 'Mankind was one Nation and Allah sent Messengers with glad tidings and warnings; and with then He sent the Book of truth, to judge between people in matters wherein they differed.' (2:213)

Ibn Kathir, the Islamic scholar and commentator on the Qur'an, mentions a disagreement between Muslim scholars on the meaning of this verse, in regard to the people who were described by God as '*Umma*', i.e. 'nation'. Some took them to be those people who lived between the times of Adam and Noah. As for what was meant by the Book, they thought it referred to the Torah that was given to the Children of Israel: 'We gave Moses the Book and followed him up with a succession of Apostles.' (2:87)

Although the People of the Book are united in their rejection of polytheism and idol worship, they disagree on other matters; such as the resurrection of the dead, in the case of the Jews, who did not accept Jesus as the Messiah. On the other hand, Muslims do not believe in the crucifixion of Jesus, nor do they agree that he was the son of God. However, in spite of these disagreements between Muslims and the People of the Book, the Qur'an confirms that there must be no conflict or clash between them because of these differences. According to Islamic teaching, both God and Muhammad have ordered believers to speak kindly to the People of the Book in their disputes. This is because the message which was given to the Prophet of Islam is regarded to be the same monotheistic message that had been given to them. People of every faith should be left to their beliefs. Thus the Qur'an instructs Muslims, saying: 'And do not dispute with the followers of the Book except by what is best, except those of them who act unjustly, and say: "We believe in that which has been revealed to us and revealed to you, and our God and your God is One, and to Him do we submit." ' (29:46)

Also: 'And there are, certainly, among the people of the Scripture (Jews and Christians), those who believe in God and in that which has been revealed to you, and in that which has been revealed to them, humbling themselves before God. They do not sell the Verses of God for a little price, for them is a reward with their Lord. Surely, God is Swift in account.' (3:199)

Muslims believe the Qur'an to be the completion of the scriptures, and to synthesise it as God's true, final, and eternal message to humanity. Because the People of the Book recognise the God of Abraham as the one and only god, in the same way as Muslims do, and practice revealed faiths based on divine ordinances, tolerance and autonomy is accorded to them in societies governed by *sharia* (Islamic divine law).

The Dhimmis

After the death of the Prophet, the Muslim caliphs extended the borders of the Islamic state outside the Arabian Peninsula. In the countries they invaded, they found many Jews and Christians of the People of the Book, and gave them special treatment as they regarded them as Dhimmis. *Dhimmi* is an idiom in Islamic jurisprudence, indicating those with whom it is permitted to conclude security agreements. These are the People of the Book, Jews and Christians, as well as Magi. This special treatment means a commitment to let the People of the Book live in Islamic lands, and give them protection, in return for the payment of the *jizya* (tribute).

The Dhimmis were allowed to run their own internal affairs by themselves, according to the Qur'anic statement: 'Let the People of the Gospel judge by what Allah hath revealed therein. If any do fail to judge by (the light of) what Allah hath revealed, they are (no better than) those who rebel.' (5:47) Legally speaking, the main condition for the presence of the Dhimmis in the Islamic state and their enjoyment of its protection was their payment of tribute. There were six conditions for Dhimma contract:

1 Not to mention Islam, either in terms of slander or praise.
2 Not to mention God's Book – the Qur'an – in terms of slander or distortion.
3 Not to mention Muhammad in terms of denial or contempt.
4 Not to marry or commit adultery with a Muslim woman.
5 Not to seduce a Muslim away from his faith or interfere with his blood or property.
6 Not to assist warmongers against the Islamic authority.

[Qasim Abdo, *Ahl Adh-Dhimma in Egypt from the Islamic Conquest to the End of the Mamluks*, p. 24]

Tribute

Scholars of Islamic Shari'a law regarded the tribute imposed on the Dhimmis as a defence tax in return for the protection they enjoyed in Islamic societies. In their view, this tax was different to the Roman poll tax. The Islamic scholar Abu Hanifa divided tribute payers into three sections: the rich, who had to pay forty-eight dirhams; the middle class, who had to pay twenty-four dirhams; and the poor, who paid only twelve dirhams. (Ibid., p. 26) Tribute should not be imposed on a child, a woman, a madman or a bisexual; neither should it be imposed on someone who was incapable of fighting, such as an old man.

Under Islamic law, the Dhimmis' properties were not subject to any tax other than tribute. As for trade, while internal trade was exempt from tax, tax on external trade had to be paid at 5 per cent. (Ibid., p. 28) Ibn Al-Hakam, the Egyptian historian of the early Islamic period, states that the tax system in Egypt remained the same after the Islamic invasion as it had been during Byzantine times. He says that Amr ibn al-'As confirmed the same taxation terms for Egypt as were levied in Roman times. (Ibn Abdul Hakam, *Futuhat Mir*, p. 70–1) Egypt was regarded as an important source of income for the Islamic caliphate in Medina, Damascus and Baghdad.

In general, Muslim rulers did not impose any bonds on the Dhimmis in their freedom of worship, and it is believed that the Umayyad Caliph Umar ibn Abdul Aziz was the first to exempt bishops and churches from paying tribute. Later, in the time of the Abbasid Caliph Al-Mu'taz, Bishop Shenoda of Alexandria sent a message to him in Baghdad, complaining that some churches had been destroyed as a result of abuse by tribute collectors. Al-Mu'taz wrote a decree ordering their rebuilding, however he died before signing it and it was left for his successor Al-Musta'in Billah to do that. (Qasim Abdo, *Ahl Adh-Dhimma*, p. 33)

The Umayyad Caliphate showed great tolerance towards the Dhimmis, giving them freedom of worship and preserving their churches. They were also treated with much tolerance during the rule of the Abbasids, while monasteries, churches and Jewish temples flourished to such an extent that early in the ninth century, under al-Ma'mun, there were more than eleven thousand churches, and several hundred monasteries within the Islamic state. In the tenth century, the Dhimmis were left to run their own affairs under their own chosen leaders. They also had their own laws and judges, while being allowed to join public posts. Soon Dhimmis became doctors, public nurses, bankers, cashiers and wholesalers. Some were even government ministers. In the mid-eleventh century, Christians held some of the highest posts in the state.

Egypt, which had been converted to Christianity for about five centuries before the arrival of Islam, was the largest Arab Christian country to fall under the Islamic caliphate. Here Muslim historians have left us a good record of the changes that took place in this home of ancient civilisation under Islamic rule.

25

Egypt before Islam

Although the term 'Copts' now indicates '*Christian* Egyptians', the Copts, generally speaking, are the descendants of the ancient Pharaonic Egyptians. Originally, this term meant native Egyptians, and it carried no religious connotation. The English word 'Copt' is itself derived from the Greek *Aiguptious,* an adjective formed from the noun *Aiguptos* (Egypt), which means 'Egyptians'. On the other hand, while the Bible identifies the country of Egypt as *Misreem* or *Misra-yim,* the Qur'an calls it *Misr*. Nevertheless, the Arabs called the inhabitants of the country *Qibt* (i.e. Copt). However, after their conquest of the country in AD 641, this term gradually became used to indicate only the Christian population, while the Egyptians as a whole became known as *Masriyeen*.

The end of pharaonic rule

After more than three thousand years of pharaonic rule, Egypt fell under Roman domination in 31 BC, following the destruction of its ships at the port of Actium on the western coast of Greece. Cleopatra VII and Mark Anthony had gone out at the head of the Egyptian navy, hoping to surprise the Roman army under Octavius by the Italian coast and defeat Rome. Octavius, however, knew of their plan and, instead of being surprised by Cleopatra and Anthony, he surprised them at their hiding place and destroyed their ships. This battle at Actium changed the course of history, leaving the road open for Rome's army to enter Alexandria. When Octavius came to the Egyptian capital, he found that Mark Anthony had already committed suicide. Soon after, Anthony was followed by Cleopatra, the last of the Ptolemaic Dynasty, with whose death the rule of the pharaohs came to an end in 30 BC.

The main interest of the Roman Emperors in Egypt was to collect tax, which was represented by a large amount of cereals to be sent yearly to Rome. To guard their new possession, the Romans left three military garrisons in Egypt, later reduced to two, each with six thousand men. From then onwards Egypt was ruled by a prefect sent by the Romans, who resided in Alexandria. Although pharaonic customs and traditions still continued, major changes took place especially in religion, language and art. Under Roman rule, ancient Egyptian polytheistic religion with multiple gods, sacred animals and images eventually died out, after about three thousand years with little change, and conversions to Christianity spread all over the country from Alexandria to Aswan.

On the other hand, although Greek continued to be the official language for the government, the mode of writing Egyptian language – in hieroglyphic, hieratic and demotic – was also replaced by a new alphabetic script, Coptic writing, using the Greek alphabet supplemented by seven special characters derived from the hieroglyphs. Meanwhile, in the field of art, the rigid classical styles of pharaonic art were replaced by more realistic forms, which we will examine in detail later.

Roman persecution – Martyr's Day

Since its establishment, the Church of Alexandria had faced successive waves of Roman persecution, either when Rome was still pagan or later when it converted to Christianity. The first official persecution carried out by the Roman authorities against the Egyptian Copts took place during the reign of Emperor Decius, who ruled Rome from 249 to 251, in an attempt to force them to make offerings to pagan gods and show that they were not Christians. However, Roman persecution of the Copts reached its zenith during the reign of Emperor Diocletian, whose coronation in 284 marked the beginning of the Coptic calendar, because of the large number of martyrs under this emperor. In that year, the Copts issued their calendar, known as the Calendar of the Martyrs, which is still celebrated today as the Nowruz, the Coptic New Year.

Less than thirty years later in 313, the Roman Empire accepted Christianity, following Emperor Constantine's 'declaration of Milan', which stipulated that Christianity had become the official religion of the Roman Empire. Thereafter, conflict between the Roman authorities and Egypt only increased. Although Egypt had been defeated by Rome, Alexandria remained its religious and cultural capital. Now the bishops of Rome wanted their city to be the religious as well as political capital of the empire. Following the Milan declaration, the bishops of Rome were granted legal authority, which enabled them to use the power of the state, including the police and army, to impose their own teaching on anyone who disagreed with them, anywhere in the empire. In AD 391, during the reign of Emperor Theodosius I, Bishop Theophilus marched from his headquarters in the Royal quarter of Alexandria, and completely destroyed the temple of Serapis in the heart of the Egyptian quarter of Rhakotis. The Serapeum, which had been the centre of Egyptian worship for seven centuries, also housed the library of Alexandria.

Byzantium

With the death of Emperor Theodosius I in 395, Rome's rule over Egypt came to an end, replaced by the Byzantine Empire, with its capital at Constantinople. From the start, relations between Egyptian Copts and the Byzantine rulers were bad; it became even worse following the Chalcedon Council in 451. This council declared that Jesus Christ's nature was dual, being fully God and fully human. This view was regarded as the true (Orthodox) belief, and anyone who disagreed on this became regarded as a heretic. The Coptic Church was one of these, and it was for this reason that the dissenting churches, headed by the Church of Alexandria, broke off from the rest of the Church at that time.

Eventually Constantinople imposed its control over the Alexandrian Church of Mark, appointing its own bishop. However, this did not succeed in subjecting the Copts, who then established their own Church of Mark away from Alexandria, and chose an Egyptian bishop to lead it. Thus Egypt had two churches for St Mark under Byzantine rule.

In an attempt to force them to accept the Roman doctrine, the Byzantine authorities started a series of persecutions against Egyptian Copts, which lasted for about two centuries before the arrival of Amr ibn al-'As in Egypt in 641. Some time before the Muslims' arrival, the emperor of Constantinople had appointed a man known in Islamic sources as Al-Muqawqis to be governor, army commander and bishop of Alexandria, so that he would have full authority in imposing the Roman doctrine on the Egyptian people. Nevertheless, the Copts refused to accept military rule for the church, and chose for themselves a bishop called Benyamin, who was forced to move secretly between the desert monasteries to avoid being captured by the Byzantines.

26

The Coptic Church

The Egyptian Coptic Church is the oldest Christian church in the world, going back to around AD 42. According to Bishop Eusebius of Caesarea, as well as Coptic traditions St Mark, the evangelist who wrote the earliest of the four New Testament gospels, was the founder and first bishop of the Church of Alexandria, even before the Church of Rome was established. In his landmark *History of the Church*, written in Greek about the year 310, Eusebius writes: 'Now, *they say* that this Mark was the first to have set out to Egypt to preach the gospel, which he had already written down, and the first to have organised churches in Alexandria itself.' This information is supplemented by Eusebius's *Chronicle*, where he places Mark's arrival in Alexandria in the third year of Claudius' reign, which would be AD 41–2 or 43–4, no more than ten years after the date fixed for the death of Christ, traditionally held to be in AD 33.

Meanwhile, the traditional Egyptian account of the history of the early Coptic Church agrees with Eusebius on Mark's role as the founder of the Alexandrian Church. However, Sawirus ibn al-Muqaffa gives a slightly later date to Mark's arrival at Alexandria: 'In the fifteenth year after the Ascension of Christ (*c.*AD 48), the holy Peter sent St Mark, the father and evangelist, to the city of Alexandria, to announce the good tiding (Gospel) there.' (Sawirus ibn al-Muqaffa, *History of the Patriarchs of the Coptic Church of Alexandria*, p. 140) The *History of the Patriarchs* attributed to Sawirus ibn al-Muqaffa is actually a multi-generational compendium of Egyptian church history that relies on several early Coptic sources, which was redacted and translated into Arabic in the eleventh century.

More information on Mark's life in Egypt is found in the Coptic account recorded by Sawirus, which is believed to have come from an earlier source. This source, known as the *Acts of Mark,* gives more details about Mark's activities in Egypt, including the account of the evangelist's martyrdom in Alexandria. The *Acts of Mark* has collected some early oral traditions and set them within a larger narrative describing the details of Mark's mission and martyrdom in Alexandria. While the exact date of composition for the *Acts of Mark* is uncertain, these traditions are traceable at least to the late fourth or early fifth century. The *Acts* incorporates two streams of tradition within a single narrative. The first stream concerns Mark's founding of the church in Alexandria. The second stream concerns Mark's martyrdom, and provides an explanation for the establishment of his martyr church on the outskirts of Alexandria.

The document was originally written in Greek and Coptic, and was rendered into several other languages. The main line of the story in the *Acts of Mark* goes like this: when the apostles were sent out in their missions, Mark received as his lot the country of Egypt and its surrounding territories. He went first to Cyrene in Libya (a second version makes him a native of Cyrene), where he did marvellous works and converted many to the Christian faith. While in Cyrene, Mark received a vision that he should go to Alexandria.

He arrived in Alexandria the next day and came to a place called Mendion. As he was entering the gate of the city, the strap of his sandal broke, and Mark looked for a cobbler to fix it. While the cobbler was working on the sandal, he injured his left hand and cried out in pain, 'God is one.' Mark healed the cobbler's hand in the name of Jesus Christ. To show his gratitude, the cobbler invited Mark to his home for a meal. There Mark began to preach the gospel of Jesus Christ, son of God, telling the man of the prophecies related to Christ. The cobbler said that he did not know of these writings, though he was familiar with the *Iliad* and the *Odyssey* and other things that Egyptians learned from childhood. The man was eventually converted, and he and his whole household were baptised, and many others besides. The cobbler's name was Ananias (the other version has Anianus).

Eventually, some pagan 'men of the city', angered by these conversions sought to kill Mark. The evangelist, decided to leave Alexandria and go back to Pentapolis, in North Africa. However, before leaving he ordained for the church Ananias (Anianus) as bishop, along with three presbyters (Milaius, Sabinus, and Cerdo).

After a two-year absence, Mark returned to Alexandria to find that the Christian community there had flourished, and a church had been built in a place called Boukolou, near the sea. However, the pagans of the city were very angry at Mark for all of his mighty works. That year, the Easter celebration occurred on the same day as a festival for the Egyptian god Serapis (24 April). A pagan group entered the church, seized Mark at the service, put a rope around his neck, and dragged him through the streets of Alexandria, until his flesh was falling from his bones. That evening, they threw him into a prison. During the night Mark was visited first by an angel and then by Christ himself, receiving words of encouragement. The next morning, the mob took Mark from prison and dragged him again through the city until he died. They then built a fire in the place called Angeloi and tried to burn Mark's body on it, but a great storm arose, and the pagan crowds fled in terror. Finally, the faithful took Mark's body and brought it back to be buried in the church, in the eastern outskirts of Alexandria.

The tradition of Mark's martyrdom at Alexandria spread all over the Roman Empire, especially in Italy, and many Christians travelled to Egypt in order to visit the Evangelist's tomb in Eastern Alexandria.

> The most important of the early Christian holy places in Alexandria was undoubtedly Boukolou, where, according to the *Acts of Mark,* the earliest Christians had their place of worship and where the saint met his death and was buried. Here was erected the *martyrium* of St Mark, attested from the late fourth century on . . . [Epiphanius refers to it as 'the church of *Baukalis*',] which I take to be a corruption, or variant, of Boukolos . . . there is no doubt that the memorial to St Mark was located in the north-eastern part of town ('in the eastern district', 'beside the

sea, beneath the cliffs'), probably near the site of the present College of St Mark run by the Christian Brothers. By the fourth century, when our documentation begins, the area in question was outside the city, a place for 'cow pastures.' But in the first century this area was the main Jewish neighbourhood, described by Josephus.

[Birger A. Pearson, 'Early Christianity in Egypt', in Birger A. Pearson & James E. Goehring (eds), *The Roots of Egyptian Christianity,* Fortress Press, Philadelphia, 1986, p. 153]

One of the earliest testimonies relating to the *martyrium* of St Mark in Alexandria, apart from the *Acts,* is found in the poetry of St Paulinus. St Paulinus of Nola (*c.*352–431), south of Rome on Italy's west coast, was ordained a priest at Christmas in 395 and became bishop of Nola in 409. As well as being a prominent Christian poet, he provides the earliest external witness to the tradition about Mark's martyrdom in Alexandria. In one of his poems, he mentions Mark's conflict with the cult of Serapis in Alexandria, a conflict that led to his imprisonment and death:

> On you, Alexandria, Mark was conferred . . . so that Egypt would not stupidly worship cattle under the name of Apis; (the holy animal of Serapis worshipped in Alexandria) . . . Satan has also fled from Egypt, where he had taken countless forms and countless names appropriate to different monsters. Thus he fashioned holy Joseph into Serapis, hiding that revered name beneath a name of death.
>
> [*The Poems of St Paulinus of Nola,* translated by P. G. Walsh, Newman Press, New York, 1975, p. 134]

Eventually, in the ninth century, according to a legend, two or three ambitious merchants from Venice were able to smuggle Mark's remains from his tomb in Alexandria. In 828, Mark replaced St Teodora, the first patron saint of Venice, where a new basilica was built for him.

27

Egyptian Monasticism

Monastic asceticism, the historical movement that transformed the early Christian world and created medieval society, originated in the Egyptian countryside. It is generally known and agreed that the Christian ascetic system of monasticism originated in Egypt; there has, however, been much dispute and disagreement regarding the date of its appearance. Egypt was the Motherland of Christian monasticism, which began even before Christianity was legalised by Constantine the Great in AD 313. The common view now is that Christian monasticism started in the last decades of the third century, around AD 270. The simple teaching of the first Egyptian monks and hermits fixed once and forever the broad outlines of the science of the spiritual life, or, in other words, of ascetic theology. It sprang into existence in the middle of the third century, and in a very few years spread over the whole Christian world.

Monasticism developed out of primitive Christian asceticism along various lines; the anchoritic and coenobitic types were the forms on which others patterned themselves. Ascetic is the term usually employed for those who in pre-monastic days forsook the world so far as they were able. Christian monasticism (from the Greek word *monachos*, which means 'solitary') refers to those Christians who seek to live a life rigorously and fully devoted to prayer, contemplation and worship. A key element in monasticism is the idea of renouncing the world and living a life of asceticism or self-denial. In medieval times, monasticism developed into a separate institution, establishing and regulating the ascetical social conditions of the manner of religious life, lived in common or in contemplative solitude. The monks brought to the Catholic Church an ideal of asceticism, forms of prayer such as the use of the Psalter, a rich experience of inwardness, and new literary forms.

St Anthony

The first chapter in the history of monasticism in Egypt is the life of St Anthony, who became the father of the monks. St Anthony went out into the wilderness to practice solitary ascetic Christianity in 271, and organised a form of monastic life for his disciples about twenty years later. Most of what we know about Anthony comes from the writings of St Athanasius the Apostolic, his disciple and close friend. Anthony was born about AD 251 to a well-to-do Coptic family from Kemn-el-Arouse (Coma) in Middle Egypt. His parents died when he was eighteen, leaving him sole guardian of his younger sister Dious. Six months later, while attending a church, he heard the scripture passage of Jesus and the rich young man, in which Jesus says, 'If you would be perfect, go, sell all you have, give to the poor, and follow me.' (Matt. 19:21)

He took this saying as a personal invitation and sold most of his inherited property, giving much of the money to the poor and the rest to his sister. After a time of study, Anthony began living in a cave, in the manner of a mountain hermit, and praying for the salvation of the world. At the age of thirty-five, he moved to Pispir and remained there in solitude for twenty years. During that time, many people came to live near him and copy his way of life, and he became their spiritual leader, teaching them the life of the ascetic. When in the early fourth century the persecutions began again against the Christians in Egypt at the hands of Maximinus Daia, Anthony went to Alexandria and ministered to those in prison. As soon as the persecutions had come to an end, he returned to his life of solitude.

Anthony did not establish any formal monastery, and his Rule was simply work and prayer. Nevertheless, he designed the first monastic uniform, an all-purpose robe of white linen fastened about the waist with a sturdy leather belt, which has become the basic pattern for monastic garb all over the world and in all times since. When St Anthony died in 356, at the age of one hundred and five, two types of monasticism were flourishing in Egypt. There were villages or colonies of hermits – the eremitical type – and monasteries in which a community life was led – the coenobitic type. St Anthony's Monastery, founded in the Egyptian desert, still exists today, and many monks still carry out his work there.

St Pachomius

A generation or so after St Anthony had started his monastic community, like-minded monks and nuns came together to form communities for mutual support and encouragement. This second form of monasticism is called coenobitic or communal monasticism, and is the more familiar form of monasticism. It arose further to the south in Upper Egypt, near present-day Luxor. A younger contemporary of Anthony, an ex-soldier named Pachomius, believed that he had received a command from heaven to build a monastery. He began organising coenobitic together in a community *c.* 320, while his sister Mary established a monastery for women nearby.

Pachomius was born in the Thebaid in Upper Egypt and as a young man was a soldier in the Roman army. In 313, Constantine was at war with Magentas; Pachomius, still a heathen, was forcibly enlisted together with a number of other young men, and placed on board a ship to be carried down the Nile to Alexandria. At some town at which the ship touched, the recruits were overwhelmed with the kindness of the Christians. Pachomius at once resolved to be a Christian and carried out his resolution as soon as he was dismissed from military service. Three years later, at the age of twenty-two, he began as an ascetic in a small village, taking up his abode in a deserted temple of Serapis and cultivating a garden on the produce of which he lived and gave alms.

Pachomius created the Coenobitic Rule, which balanced the communal life and the solitary life, a Rule that became the basis for almost every monastic order to come, especially that of St Benedict, who based his famous order almost entirely on the Pachomian Rule. St Jerome, famous for translating the Bible into Latin, also translated Pachomius' Rule, which is still used by many monasteries today. Pachomius realised that a community of monks working together could accomplish more, both for themselves and society, than hermits living in isolation. In coenobitic monasticism, the monks live in a communal environment, each one working for the betterment of the whole. Coenobitic monasteries are entirely self-sufficient, with farms and herds, plus libraries, hospitals, and kitchens in which every monk works. St Pachomius founded his first monastery in Tabenna near Denderah around 323, and by the time of his death in 346 during a plague, he had under him eight or nine large monasteries of men, and two of women of five or ten thousand nuns and monks.

St Pachomius and coenobites in general place a greater emphasis on prayer, as well as the importance of manual labour to support the community. A Pachomian monastery was an industrial community in which almost every kind of trade was practised. This, of course, involved much buying and selling, so the monks had ships of their own on the Nile, which conveyed their agricultural produce and manufactured goods to the market and brought back what the monasteries required. The monastery was a collection of buildings surrounded by a wall. The monks were distributed in houses, each house containing about forty monks. Three or four houses constituted a tribe. There could be thirty to forty houses in one monastery. Presiding over each monastery were an abbot and provosts, with subordinate officials for each house. The monks were divided into houses according to the work they did: thus there would be a house for carpenters, a house for agriculturists, and so forth. On Saturdays and Sundays all the monks assembled in the church for Mass. According to St Jerome, in the preface to his translation of the 'Rule of Pachomius', the tables were laid twice a day except on Wednesdays and Fridays, which, outside the seasons of Easter and Pentecost, were fast days. Some took very little at the second meal; some confined themselves to a single food at one or other of the meals; others took just a morsel of bread.

With the exception of a single Pachomian monastery at Canopus, near Alexandria, the coenobitic monasteries were confined to a relatively small area in the South. The eremitical monasteries, on the contrary, were found everywhere, and especially in the North. The latter were thus far more accessible to pilgrims visiting Egypt and so became the patterns or models for the rest of the Christian world. It was the eremitical, not the coenobitical, type of monasticism which went forth from Egypt.

The spread of Monasticism

Within Egypt, monasticism spread along the route of the Israelite Exodus and the desert of the Forty Years' Wandering. The attraction of Mount Sinai for the solitaries was irresistible, in spite of the danger of captivity or death at the hands of the Saracens. In Palestine, St Hilarion, who for a time had been a disciple of St Anthony, propagated monasticism of the eremitical type first in the neighbourhood of his native city Gaza and then in Cyprus. His friend, St Epiphanius, after practising the monastic life in Egypt, founded a monastery near Eleutheropolis in Palestine in around 330. However, when Athanasius wrote the biography of St Anthony, it became instrumental in spreading the monastic idea throughout the Christian world. The knowledge of the monastic life was carried to Western Europe by St Athanasius of Alexandria, who in 340 went to Rome accompanied by two monks.

Monasticism soon became common in Rome and throughout Italy, and before long spread to Gaul and North Africa. Soon Monasticism spread over the whole of the eastern half of the Roman Empire in the fourth century. Athanaius's *Life of Anthony* (*c*.357) became a Christian classic in his lifetime. In Constantinople, the capital of the later Roman Empire, monasticism established itself *c*.380; although its original contacts were with Syria, it manifested Egyptian influence when the Origentist monks were expelled by Theophilus of Alexandria *c*.400. By 518 there were already at least fifty-four monasteries in Constantinople. At the Council of Chalcedon in 451, monasticism had become part of the life of the Church that it was specially legislated for. It was decided that monasteries were not to be erected without the permission of the bishop. Although monks were to receive due honour, they were not to mix themselves up with the affairs of Church or State and were to be subject to the bishop.

28

The Arab Conquest of Egypt

It was Amr ibn al-'As, the commander of the Arab troops, who first thought of conquering Egypt. Amr had been to Egypt for trade many times before Islam, and knew how rich the country was. When Caliph Umar came to the Levant in 639 on his way to receive the keys of Jerusalem from its Bishop, Amr offered him a plan to conquer Egypt. Umar hesitated in accepting Amr's plan, fearing that the Arab troops would be too exhausted by continuous fighting. Amr, however, did not give up and continued to argue the importance of Egypt, telling the caliph how rich the country was and how easy it would be for him to conquer, until at last Umar allowed him to march to Egypt.

At the time of the Arab invasion in the seventh century, Egypt was part of Byzantium. (This was the time of Emperor Heraclius, whose viceroy was residing in Alexandria.) However, the main Byzantine force was stationed at the fortress of Babilyon on the eastern bank of the Nile, near modern Cairo, with a chain of smaller fortress towns running across the country. From these towns, soldiers and tax-gatherers patrolled the country, keeping order and collecting money.

Amr battles with the Byzantine Romans

In December 639 Amr left Caesarea on the Palestinian coast for Egypt, with only 4,000 fighters. He arrived with his army to the border town of El Arish, where there was no Byzantine garrison, and the citizens offered no resistance. Having spent the Greater Bairam there, Amr then marched west away from the Mediterranean coast, following the same ancient road between Egypt and the

Levant. The Muslim army reached Pelusium in northern Sinai, a fortified town manned by a Byzantine garrison, which contained many ancient Egyptian monuments, as well as some Christian churches and monasteries. The city had been a Pharaonic port by the village of Baluzah, thirty-five kilometres to the east of Qantara. It had a harbour and strong fortifications, and was connected with the rest of the country through a Nile stream.

The Muslim army had to impose a blockade on Pelusium for about a month before it opened its doors in February 640. Arab historians state that the local Copts helped the Arab army in achieving this victory. According to Jamaluddin Abul-mahasin ibn Taghry, in his book *Annujoom Azzahirah fi Mulook Mir wal Qahirah* (The Shining Stars):

> Amr came until he was at Al-Arish and the first location for him to confront fighting was at Farama (Pelusium). The Byzantines fought him heavily for about a month, then God opened (the city) by his hands. Amr then marched to the city of Belbeis in the Eastern Delta, and imposed a siege on it for a whole month. After a fierce battle with Byzantine forces, Amr was able to capture the city. Then the road was open for him to reach the fort of Babilyon near modern Cairo, where the main Byzantine forces were gathered.

The Fort of Babilyon

Amr continued his march until he reached a village on the Nile north of Babilyon Fort, whose modern location lies in central Cairo by Azbakiya Parkas; at the time, the Nile reached this area. Babilyon was a larger and more important city, close to Memphis, the ancient capital of the Pharaohs, and near modern Cairo. The Byzantines then realised the seriousness of the situation and gathered at the fort to organise their defence. The Muslim troops arrived before Fort Babilyon some time in May 640, while they were preparing themselves for a long siege, digging a ditch outside the city and placing a large force in the area between the ditch and the city walls.

The Fort of Babilyon was a massive structure 60 ft. high with walls more than 6 ft. thick and studded with numerous towers and bastions. When Amr arrived at the fort, he formed up his force of 4,000 men in assault formation and started to attack the Byzantine positions, but his attack was repulsed. Amr then pulled his men back and marched west towards the bank of the Nile, turning south to the Fayyum. The Byzantines had anticipated this raid on the Fayyum, and thus strongly guarded the roads leading to it. Failing to invade Fayyum, Amr withdrew to the desert and sent to Caliph Umar, asking for more troops.

When the new forces of four thousand fighters arrived at the battle front in the late summer, Amr was ready to resume fighting. The new force comprised four columns, each column was one thousand strong and commanded by its own commander, while Zubair ibn al-Awam, a renowned warrior and commander, veteran of the Battle of Yarmouk and once part of Khalid ibn Walid's elite force mobile guard, was appointed the supreme commander of the army. Other commanders were Miqdad bin Al-Aswad; Ubaida bin As-Samit, and Kharija bin Huzafa.

When the Arab forces were able to dominate the northern section of Babilyon Fort, about sixty acres of present day Old Cairo, the Byzantine army went out after them to cut off their road in the valley stretching between the Fort and Heliopolis (Ayn Shams). However, the Muslim high command set up an ambush for the Byzantines and inflicted heavy casualties on them by encircling the troops from three sides. Though the Byzantines were able to retreat back to the fort, they became too weak to launch any other offensive.

Realising his inability to resist the Arab attack, Cyrus, the Byzantine governor of Egypt, who is known as *Maquaqas* in Muslim sources, escaped from the fort to the Nile Isle of Rauda, from where he entered into peace negotiations with the invaders. Amr, however, asked the Byzantines to pay a ransom. Cyrus entered into a treaty with the Muslims, by which Muslim sovereignty over the whole of Egypt was recognised, and the Coptic Egyptians agreed to pay *jizya* tax at the rate of two dinars per male adult. The treaty was subject to the approval of the emperor Heraclius, but Cyrus stipulated that even if the emperor repudiated the treaty, he and the Copts would honour the terms of the treaty, recognise the supremacy of the Muslims and pay them *jizya*.

Heraclius refused to accept the treaty negotiated by his viceroy, and Cyrus waited on Amr and told him that Heraclius had repudiated the treaty of Babilyon, assuring him that so far as the Copts were concerned the terms of the treaty would be followed. It is reported that Cyrus asked for three favours from the Muslims, namely:

1. Do not break your treaty with the Copts;
2. If the Byzantines after this repudiation ask for peace, do not make peace with them, but treat them as captives and slaves; and
3. When I am dead allow me to be buried in the Church of St John at Alexandria.

The takeover of Alexandria

Following the emperor's refusal of the peace agreement, the Muslims resumed fighting. In a moonless December night, Zubair and some of his warriors managed to scale the wall, killing the guards and opening the gates for the Muslim army to enter. Thus the fortified city of Babilyon was captured by the Muslims on 21 December 640. In February 641, Amr set off from Babilyon to Alexandria with his army. He arrived before the heavily fortified city in March 641 and laid siege. The Byzantine commanders had expected that after Babilyon the Muslims' next target would be Alexandria, and prepared for the siege to be laid on the city. Their strategy was to keep the Muslims away by destroying their power through continued sallies and attacks from the fort. There were walls behind walls and forts within forts, and the city had direct access to the sea, with an open route for help to arrive from Constantinople. The Byzantines had high stakes in Alexandria, and they were determined to offer stiff resistance to the Muslims. They mounted catapults on the walls of the city, which pounded the Muslim positions with boulders. This caused considerable damage to the Arab troops, so Amr ordered his men back from the advanced position.

It is said that Heraclius intended to sail from Constantinople to

Alexandria with a large reinforcement. However, he died before he could carry out his plan. When the siege of Alexandria had dragged on for six months, Caliph Umar in Medina became impatient. In a letter addressed to Amr, the caliph expressed his concern at the delay in the invasion of Egypt. He further instructed that the new field commander would be Ubada, and he would launch the assault at the fort of Alexandria. Ubada's assault was successful and Alexandria was captured by Muslims in September 641. Thousand of Byzantine soldiers were killed or taken captive while other managed to flight to Constantinople through ships that stood anchored in the port. In his report to Caliph Umar after the fall of Alexandria, Amr wrote:

> I have opened the city . . . it has four thousand buildings with four thousand baths, forty thousand Jews who have to pay tribute, four hundred royal places of entertainment and twelve thousand shops that sell green vegetables . . . There were two hundred thousand Romans in the city, who went to their land by sea. It (Alexandria) had one hundred large boats, which took thirty thousand (of the Romans), with what they could carry of family and possession. Those who remained, who have reached the age of tribute excluding boys and women, were counted as one thousand.
>
> [*Futuh Misr*, p. 82]

Amr wanted to remain at Alexandria and make it his capital, as it had been the since the beginning of the Ptolemaic rule about nine centuries earlier. However, when Umar refused his demand, Amr moved Egypt's capital from Alexandria to Fustat, near Babilyon Fort, and within two years all of Egypt had become part of the Islamic Empire. The Arabs declared their pledge of the freedom of worship for the People of the Book, Christians and Jews. Following the departure of the Byzantines, they brought the Coptic Bishop Benyamin I out from hiding and delivered the churches of Alexandria to him. The bishop, who had spent a large part of his life in struggle against the Byzantines, started to strengthen the Jacobean Church and re-establish the monasteries and churches which had been destroyed before Islamic invasion. Benyamin also sent a new archbishop to Abyssinia, and his last work was the establishing of a new church for St Makarious in Wadi Natroun in the western desert.

According to Ibn Al-Hakam, in his book about the invasion of Egypt and its story, there were two hundred thousand Byzantine Romans in Alexandria, the strongest of whom left to their land by sea. There were a hundred large ships waiting at Alexandria, which carried thirty thousand of them, with whatever they could take of relatives and possessions. All those who were left behind, six hundred thousand men, as well as women and children, had to pay tribute. The Muslim fighters demanded their share of the booty. Amr wrote to the Caliph Umar asking him what to do. Umar wrote back to him telling him to ignore their demand and send the tribute to Medina to be for all Muslims, strength for their struggle.

Amr, who confirmed Umar's demands, counted the number of people in Egypt, and imposed tribute on each one of them; every man in Egypt should pay two dinars. As Alexandria had been taken by force and had no conciliation of security, its inhabitants should pay a proportion of their wages, while the inhabitants of the villages that had fought on the side of the Byzantines were taken captives as slaves of war. However, Amr soon sent them back to their villages, and let them free, imposing tribute on them, making them Ahl Dhimma with the Copts. *Jizya* (tribute) is a sum of money which had to be paid by non-Muslims as tax, which was dropped for those who converted to Islam, while *Kharaj* was a land tax fixed only on the cultivated land, and was not reduced with conversion to Islam.

Copts welcome Amr bin Al-'as in Egypt

After six centuries of suffering under Roman and Byzantine rule, very few Egyptians were ready to support the Byzantines, and the sympathies of the Copts were now by and large with the Muslims. As they could not take part in fighting the Byzantines, the Copts undertook to help the Muslims in the promotion of the war effort and the provision of stores; to build roads and bridges for them; and to provide them with moral support.

29

Search for Identity

Turkey's decision to abolish the Islamic caliphate in 1924 left the Arab nations with a sense of loss, without identity. Following their defeat, Mustafa Kemal Ataturk, the first president of the Turkish Republic, decided to abolish the Ottoman caliphate in Istanbul. After thirteen centuries of Islamic rule, the caliphate, an institution which had been an organic part of Islamic life, was abolished in Constantinople. Although the countries of the Middle East had a long history before the appearance of Islam in the seventh century AD, they seem to have lost their national identity when they became part of the new Islamic Empire. Egypt, Mesopotamia, Syria, Phoenicia and Palestine, which represented the cradle of human civilisation where Judaism and Christianity had appeared hundreds of years earlier, identified themselves only as Muslim subjects of the Caliph.

With their national homelands dissolved within the dominating caliphate for about thirteen centuries, the Muslim peoples of the Arab countries were now faced with a problem of identity. As the head of the Islamic state and community, the caliph was both the political and the religious leader of the people. The caliph was regarded as the 'Successor of the Prophet' and 'the Commander of the Faithful'. For nearly 1,300 years, the caliphate had been a symbol of Muslim unity, even identity; its disappearance, under the assault of foreign imperialists during World War I, left a big vacuum in the Muslim world. Islam had become not just a faith, but a whole way of life, even a nationality. As Bernard Lewis, a Princeton professor and historian of the Middle East, has put it:

> For Muslims, Islam is not merely a system of belief and worship,

> a compartment of life, so to speak, distinct from other compartments . . . It is rather the whole of life, and its rules include civil, criminal, and even what we would call constitutional law . . . It is by now a commonplace that the term 'Islam' is the counterpart not only of 'Christianity' but also of 'Christendom'.
>
> (Bernard Lewis, *Islam and the West*, p. 3–4)

In an attempt to fill the vacuum created by the disappearance of the caliphate, two different movements appeared in the Middle East: one nationalistic, working for the independence of the Arab countries; and the other religious, hoping for the reviving of the Caliphate. Thus the birth of modern Arab nationalism is associated with the decline and fall of the Ottoman Empire, and with Arab aspirations to political independence and unity.

However, until the start of the First World War, most Arab leaders had no intention of rebelling against the Ottoman rule. Only towards the end of the nineteenth century and at the beginning of the twentieth did small groups of local patriots start to preach love of the homeland, principally in Damascus, Beirut and Cairo. Butrus al-Bustani in Beirut, Shaykh Rifa'a al-Tahtawi, and Urabi Pasha in Egypt were among those early patriots; although they did not seek the secularisation of the Muslim institutions of the Ottoman Empire or the unification of the Arab countries against the Turks. During the latter part of the nineteenth century the anti-Turkish struggle emphasised Arabism and Arab unity rather than local patriotism, particularly in the Ottoman provinces of Damascus and Beirut. A number of Arab groups and political parties were established to call for Arab unity, demanding complete autonomy for the Arab provinces of the Ottoman Empire.

When the Ottomans decided to join World War I on the side of the Central Powers against the Allies in 1914, the Allies promised the Arabs to help gain independence if they joined the war against the Ottomans. Encouraged by the Allies' promise, the Arabs started their revolt against the Ottomans under the leadership of Sharif Hussein the Hashemite ruler of Hijaz. Hussein's objective was to establish a single independent and unified Arab state, stretching from Aleppo in northern Syria to Aden in south Yemen. In his first letter to Sir Henry McMahon, the British high commissioner in Egypt, Hussein proposed that Britain should support the creation of an area of Arab independence embracing the whole of Mesopotamia, the Levant and the Arabian Peninsula with the exception of Aden, which was a British colony.

Arab nationalists in the Fertile Crescent and the Arabian Peninsula found in the Hashemite commanders of the Great Arab Revolt the leadership that could realise their aspirations in unity and independence. In June 1916, as head of the Arab nationalists and in alliance with Britain and France, Sharif Hussein initiated the Great Arab Revolt against Ottoman rule. Arab nationalist groups in Syria, Iraq and Arabia began to rally behind the Hashemite banner of Abdullah and Faysal, sons of Sharif Hussein bin Ali, King of the Arabs. At the end of the war, Arab forces controlled much of southern Syria, all of modern Jordan, and all the Hijaz of western Arabia.

Hussein was first proclaimed 'King of the Arabs' in Mecca on 30 October 1916. He later accepted the title of King of the Hijaz, in western Arabia, when the Allies refused to recognise his authority over the Levant. On 1 October 1918, Prince Faysal's victorious Arab forces entered Damascus, announcing the establishment of an independent Arab government in Syria, in the name of his father Hussein. Faysal, who had developed a rudimentary theory of Arab nationalism, was hoping to unite the Arab nations under one sovereign government, with its capital at Damascus. The General Syrian Congress established by Faysal made a historic resolution on 7 March 1920 proclaiming the full independence of a united Syria, which included Palestine and Lebanon. This was the first time for the concept of a single Arab, as opposed to Islamic, nation to appear since the establishment of the Islamic state thirteen centuries earlier.

The years 1918–20 represented a turning point in the modern history of the Arabs, when their lands were separated from the Ottoman Empire. Following the end of the war, however, the Allies reneged on their promises to Hussein; carving from the dismembered

Ottoman lands a system of mandates and protectorates. Instead of achieving their independence, soon most of the Arab provinces fell under the Western forces of Britain and France. The Arab joy at the liberation of their lands from the Ottoman yoke was short lived. The French military governor of Lebanon wasted no time to announce that he was restoring the independence of Lebanon under the protection of the French Republic. On 25 July 1920, twenty-one months and twenty-two days after Faysal's entry into Damascus, a French force occupied the Syrian city, putting an end to the Arab government and forcing the Hashemite emir to leave the city.

The period of Anglo-French imperial rule had started with the French in Algeria (1830) and the British in Aden (1839); it continued with the British occupation of Egypt (1882), the extension of French control to Tunisia (1881) and Morocco (1911), and the spread of British influence in the Gulf emirates. Following the approval of the Council of the League of Nations on 24 July 1922, of the mandates system for these countries, Britain and France divided between them the Arab provinces of Iraq, Syria, Lebanon, Transjordan and Palestine.

While the Hashemites did not seem to have abandoned their dream of establishing a pan-Arab political entity, their own position at home was undermined. In the summer of 1924, they were confronted by a serious attack on the Hijaz by a second Saudi-Wahhabi alliance which forced Hussein to abdicate his authority on 5 October in favour of his son Ali. The second alliance between the House of Saud and the Wahhabis began in the last years of the Ottoman Empire. In 1921 Sheikh Abdul-Aziz Ibn Saud was able to defeat his old rival in Northern Najd, Ibn Rashid, annexing his territories and assuming the title 'Sultan of Najd'. Having united the tribes of east and central Arabia under his control, Abdul-Aziz moved west to conquer Hijaz. Sharif Hussein, unable to face the Wahhabi attack on Mecca, handed his authority to his son Ali and left for Jedda from where he proceeded to Aqaba. Later, in July 1925, he left for Cyprus on board a British destroyer. The Wahhabis occupied Jedda, Medina and Yanbu'. A short time later, Ali Ibn

Hussein was also forced to abdicate his authority and leave for Baghdad, where he spent the rest of his life. Ali's departure cleared the way for Ibn Saud, who proclaimed himself 'King of the Hijaz and Sultan of Najd and its Dependencies' on 8 January 1926. Later, in September 1932, Ibn Saud declared a new unitary state, to be called the Kingdom of Saudi Arabia. Thus from its first day, Wahhabism became the official state-enforced doctrine of the Kingdom of Saudi Arabia, being the custodian of the two holiest places of Islam: Mecca and Medina.

At the same time, Yemen and the Gulf area remained under British control, encompassing no less than twenty rulers of various principalities and sheikhdoms: from Kuwait, at the tip of the Gulf, to Aden and the Protectorate; the island of Perim at the southern entrance of the Red Sea; passing by the island of Bahrain, Qatar, the Trucial Coast (now the United Arab Emirates), and the sultanate of Oman.

Following the failure of the Arab national movement to establish a unified Arab state in Damascus and Hussein's departure from Hijaz, a new political movement appeared in the Arab countries. The aim was to re-establish their unity, this time under the Islamic banner. A caliphate congress was held in Cairo in May 1926, with the aim of restoring the institution of the caliphate. However, the majority of the thirty-eight delegates who came from thirteen Muslim countries came to the conclusion that the restoration of the caliphate was not possible at that time, as the majority of the Muslim peoples were looking forward to their national independence. This did not, however, close the door to those who insisted on reuniting the Arab countries in one Islamic state. In 1928, a few years after the collapse of the Ottoman Caliphate, *al-Ikhwan al-Muslimeen*, the Muslim Brotherhood, was established in Egypt by Hassan el-Banna. The Brotherhood declared its objective to be 'Building the Muslim state' and 'Building the Caliphate'.

30

The Birth of Political Islam

The Muslim Brotherhood was the first Islamic political group, founded by the Egyptian schoolteacher Hassan el-Banna in 1928. The main aim of the group was to establish an Islamic government in Egypt, which would rule by Sharia Law and would eventually be able to unify other Islamic countries in a new caliphate. Although here the Brotherhood is obviously talking politics, their use of the Sharia Law was deliberately intended to confuse the issue, giving their cause a religious nature. According to Islamic belief, Sharia represents the sacred religious regulations concerning worship: prayers, fasting, pilgrimage and alms giving; as well as dealings such as marriage, divorce and inheritance. It also includes some regulations for trade and criminal activities. The Sharia rules governing these matters are regarded sacred, as they are founded on both the Qur'an and the acts and sayings of the Prophet. However, the Brotherhood did not mention these sacred Sharia rules in its declaration, as they had already been applied, not only in Egypt but in all Islamic countries.

What the Brotherhood meant by Sharia Law was the law of the Islamic state under the caliphs, which is not sacred as it was not founded on Qur'anic statements or the Prophet's Tradition. As Hassan el-Banna clearly stated, the goal of his organisation was to re-establish an empire, stretching from Spain to Indonesia. There is no single reference either in the Qur'an or the words of the Prophet to either an Islamic state or a caliphate. However, when the Islamic state emerged under the caliphs after the death of the Prophet, beginning with the reigns of Caliphs Abu Bakr (632–4) and Umar (634–44), it needed laws to regulate its newly founded government. It was then that the rulers and judges had to rely on jurisprudence (*Figh*), human law and interpretation to establish new laws. They used analogy (*Qiyas*) and consensus (*Ijma*) to establish new Sharia Laws to run the state. These laws had to deal with many aspects of life that didn't exist during Muhammad's life, including crime, politics, economics, banking, business, contracts, relations with foreign countries and social issues. In contrast with the sacred Sharia regulations founded on the Qur'an and the Prophet's teachings, these laws cannot be regarded as holy, sacred or eternal. They are man-made laws which are not part of the religious beliefs.

The Brotherhood also established a secret military wing, the secret apparatus, which began to carry out terrorist attacks inside the country soon after the end of World War II. When it decided to send its volunteers to fight the newly born state of Israel in 1948, its popularity increased and it became one of the most influential movements in Egypt. However, in December 1948, following the discovery of caches of bombs and other weapons accumulated by the apparatus, the Egyptian Prime Minister, Mahmud Fahmi el-Nokrashi, ordered the dissolution of the Brotherhood. A few weeks later, on 28 December, a Muslim brother assassinated Prime Minister Noqrashi Pasha in what is thought to have been retaliation for the government crackdown. A month and half later, on 12 February 1949, el-Banna himself was killed in Cairo by security agents. El-Banna was succeeded as head of the Brotherhood by Hassan el-Hudaybi, a former judge; he failed to control the secret apparatus, and it continued to operate without the leadership's knowledge.

When in 1952 Gamal Abdel Nasser led a military coup to overthrow the monarchy, dissolving the parliament, cancelling the 1923 constitution and forbidding all political parties, he had the backing of the Muslim Brotherhood. However, the honeymoon between Nasser and the Brotherhood did not last long and, following an assassination attempt by a member of the secret apparatus in 1954, Nasser abolished the Brotherhood, imprisoning and punishing thousands of its members. It was then that thousands of Muslim Brothers escaped from Egypt to the neighbouring Arab countries, especially Saudi Arabia, where they were welcomed and offered a safe place to live.

The Brotherhood and the Copts

In their proposed Islamic state, the Muslim Brotherhood regarded non-Muslims as *dhimmis*, who would lose the status of full citizenship which they had regained following the fall of the Ottoman Empire. In 1997 Mustafa Mashhur, the Supreme Guide of the Muslim Brotherhood, told journalist Khalid Daoud that he thought Egypt's Coptic Christians should pay the long-abandoned *jizya* poll tax levied on non-Muslims in exchange for protection from the state. He rationalised his argument by the fact that non-Muslims are exempt from military service while it is compulsory for Muslims. He went on to say: 'we do not mind having Christian members in the People's Assembly . . . the top officials, especially in the army, should be Muslims since we are a Muslim country . . . This is necessary because when a Christian country attacks the Muslim country and the army has Christian elements, they can facilitate our defeat by the enemy.' (Caryle Murphy, *Passion for Islam: Shaping the Modern Middle East: the Egyptian Experience*, Simon and Schuster, New York 2002, pp. 241, 330)

Pan-Arabism

Like Hassan el-Banna, Nasser did not believe that national boundaries should separate the different Arab countries; and he planned to form a great united state. Nevertheless, unlike the Muslim Brothers, his aim was to establish a secular Arab state, not a Muslim caliphate. Nasser believed in pan-Arabism, a movement that calls for unification among the peoples and countries of the Arab World, from the Atlantic Ocean to the Arabian Sea. When World War II drew to a close, Arab nationalist ambitions and the desire to prevent creation of a Jewish homeland in Palestine had led to the creation of the Arab League and thereafter to the rise of Arab national sentiment. Nasser, now president of Egypt, took advantage of the anti-imperialist feeling to become the leader of a pan-Arab ideology in the 1960s, which tried to unite Arabs beyond the confines of the nation states.

Soon after 1952, Nasser moved full steam ahead into the sphere of Arab nationalism and Arab unity. On 1 February 1958, the birth of the United Arab Republic, formed by the union of Egypt and Syria, was proclaimed in Cairo. This was followed almost immediately, on 14 February, by a union between the kingdoms of Iraq and Jordan. However, the latter union was soon brought to an end by the Iraqi *coup d'etat* of 14 July 1958, while Syria severed its ties with Egypt in September 1961. Following the fall of the union between Egypt and Syria, Nasser supported the revolution in Yemen, but Saudi Arabia, without whose support no hope for an Arab union can be entertained, opposed his plans. At the same time, Nasser's socialist reforms at home alienated most of the rich Gulf States from the idea of a united Arab state. Later, after Nasser's defeat in the Six Day War against Israel in 1967, Pan-Arabism declined in all Arab countries.

The failure of Pan-Arabism left political Islam as the most attractive alternative to the oppressed Arab masses. When Nasser had eliminated all opposition parties, political Islamic movements became the only refuge for the unsatisfied masses.

Islamic jihad

On the other hand, in the 60s a new more dramatic development had taken place in the ideology of political Islam, which argued that violence was the only way to bring about the Islamic state. Sayyid Qutb, an author member of the Brotherhood, wrote *Milestones* while in prison. In it, he opposed Nasser's call for Arab nationalism, and advocated an Islamic political system with no government. He argued that the Muslim world had ceased to exist, that it had in fact reverted to the pre-Islamic period of ignorance known as *jahilyyah* when it abandoned the Sharia Law of the Islamic state. Consequently, he believed that none of the Muslim states were Islamic and that they were thus illegitimate.

His suggested method of correcting this situation was the abolition of the ruling political authorities by force, or *jihad*. When a truly Islamic community was formed, it should use force to spread through the Islamic countries and then conquer the rest of the world and bring about the rule of God. Sayyid Qutb, like all Islamic terrorist groups, took the word *jihad* to mean war against non-Muslims.

This, however, is not the right interpretation of the word *jihad* as it appeared in the Qur'an. While the Prophet was still in Mecca, no Qur'anic statement was made about jihad, war or fighting the enemies. All the Qur'anic verses which talk about fighting in God's cause were delivered later in Medina. As the Quraishi Muslims, including Muhammad himself, had been forced to leave their homes and possessions in Mecca and run away to safety in Medina, they felt they must fight the Meccans in order to get compensation for what they had lost. Three main wars were fought in Medina between Muslim and Meccan armies. All the Qur'anic verses which talk about war and *jihad* were received during this period, not as general religious obligation, but as comments on specific historical events: 'To those against whom war is made, permission is given (to fight) because they are wronged . . . (They are) those who have been expelled from their homes in defiance of right, (for no cause) except that they say, "Our Lord is Allah." ' (22:39–40). Nevertheless, when the Prophet of Islam entered Mecca victorious, no single person was killed by the Muslims, despite the fact that all Meccans were still unbelievers at the time.

Qutb, who has been described as someone who shaped the ideas of terrorist groups such as al-Qa'ida, had great influence on the new jihadi Islamic groups, both in Egypt and elsewhere in the Arab countries. After his execution on 29 August 1966, his views spread outside the country. When his brother Muhammad moved to Saudi Arabia, he became a professor of Islamic Studies, who edited, published and promoted Sayyid's work. One of Muhammad Qutb's students was Ayman Zawahiri, who became a member of the Egyptian Islamic Jihad and later a mentor of Osama bin Laden and a leading member of al-Qa'ida. Bin Laden himself was also acquainted with Muhammad Qutb, and attended his weekly public lectures at King Abdulaziz University in Jeddah.

It was the marriage between the fundamental Wahhabi beliefs of Saudi Arabia and Egyptian political Islamic ideology that helped to create the many terrorist *jihadi* groups all over the world. According to Prince Naif Ibn Abdul Aziz, the Interior Minister of Saudi Arabia, the Muslim Brotherhood organisation has been the cause of most of the Arab world's problems:

> 'The Brotherhood has done great damage to Saudi Arabia,' he said. 'All our problems come from the Muslim Brotherhood. We have given too much support to this group . . . Whenever they got into difficulty or found their freedom restricted in their own countries, Brotherhood activists found refuge in the Kingdom which protected their lives . . . But they later turned against the Kingdom . . . ' The Interior Minister's outburst against the Brotherhood came amid mounting criticism in the United States of Saudi Arabia's long-standing support for Islamist groups around the world . . .
>
> [*Ain Al Yaqeen Weekly*, November 29, 2002]

31

Christians in Arab Countries

When the first Islamic empire was established about fourteen centuries ago, most of the Middle Eastern population had already been converted to Christianity. Today, only some small Christian minorities are found in countries like Lebanon, Iraq, Syria, and the Palestinian West Bank, with the Coptic Christian community in Egypt being the largest, estimated at about fifteen million.

Since the rise of political Islam over the last few decades, many Christians have emigrated from the Middle East, looking for a more secured life in the West. Christian populations in some Arab countries have come under pressure, facing persecution both in their religious and their social activities. The Assyrian International News Agency quoted the Lebanese Maronite Patriarch Nasrallah Butros Sfeir as telling French President Nicholas Sarkozy during their meeting at the Élysée Palace that 'The number of Christians in the Middle East is swiftly declining'. It also reported that 'Pope Benedict XVI had warned . . . that the Christian community in the Middle East would soon disappear if no solution to regional conflicts was found, while citing rising political Islam and its extreme currents as a threat to Christians and Muslims alike.' (17 June, 2010)

The Vatican Assembly

Pope Benedict XVI has announced a special Assembly of the Synod dedicated to the Middle East, from the 10th to the 24 October 2010. The decision to hold the meeting was in response to the desire expressed for quite some time by the Eastern Catholic Churches.

During Pope Benedict XVI's three-day visit to Greek Cyprus in the summer of 2010, a document was issued on Sunday the 5 June which cites the 'extremist current' unleashed by the rise of 'Political Islam' as a threat to Christians. The document that was written by a dozen bishops and top Vatican officials, said Christians suffered in countries where Muslims often 'make no distinction between religion and politics'. It also said that relations between Christians and Muslims were often difficult 'principally because Muslims make no distinction between religion and politics, thereby relegating Christians to the precarious position of being considered non-citizens, despite the fact that they were citizens of their countries long before the rise of Islam.'

The Assembly to be held in Rome in October 2010, will focus the attention of the international community 'on the plight of those Christians in the Middle East who suffer for their beliefs'. The Vatican, which estimates there are about 17 million Christians from Iran to Egypt, said that the international community is ignoring the plight of Christians in the Middle East, and that the Israeli–Palestinian conflict, the war in Iraq and political instability in Lebanon have forced thousands to flee the region. In recent decades, the percentage of Christians in the Middle East has fallen from 20 per cent of the population to less than 5 per cent, and the number is dropping.

As the Gulf States have almost no Christian citizens, and North Africa has only tiny Christian communities, we are going to examine the situation in the counties of the Fertile Crescent and Egypt. In Syria, while there has been no recent census taken, current estimates put the Christian population at about two million, just under 10 per cent of the total population, which is thought to have been 21,906,000 in 2009. Although some Christians live in the capital city of Damascus, the majority live in the northern city of Aleppo. However, Syrian Christians enjoy every aspect of Syrian life, participating in the economy and intellectual life as well as in their country's political arena. Many Syrian Christians are public and private sector managers and directors, local administrators, members in the Parliament, and ministers in the government. A number of them are also officers in the Syrian armed forces.

The situation in Jordan, where the Christians number about

400,000 and constitute about 7 per cent of the population as it was estimated in 2009, is even better. They are well integrated in society and have a high level of freedom. Nearly all Jordanian Christians belong to the middle or upper classes and enjoy more economic and social opportunity in the Hashemite Kingdom. They have large representation in the Jordanian parliament (10 per cent of the Parliament) and hold important government portfolios, ambassadorial appointments abroad, and positions of high military rank.

The situation in the four other countries, however, is completely different, as Christian populations in Iraq, Palestinian Gaza and the West Bank, Lebanon and Egypt have quickly deteriorated.

Iraq

Before the Gulf War in 1991, Iraqi Christians numbered about one million. Many left their country in the wake of the war, however; by the time of the US attack on Saddam Hussein in 2003, that figure had fallen further to about 800,000. Since then about half a million more Christians have been forced to flee Iraq to neighbouring countries or migrate to the West, and about a hundred thousand more have taken shelter in northern Iraq on the Plain of Nineveh. On October 2005, the United Nations High Commissioner for Refugees reported that of the 700,000 Iraqis who took refuge in Syria between October 2003 and March 2005, 36 per cent were 'Iraqi Christians'.

Most Iraqi Christians are Chaldeans, Eastern-rite Catholics who, while autonomous from Rome, recognise the Pope's authority. The other significant community are Assyrians, whose Ancient Church of the East is believed to be the oldest in Iraq. They live in Baghdad as well as the northern cities of Kirkuk, Irbil and Mosul.

Palestine

Before the establishment of the state of Israel in 1948, Arab Christians of Palestine are believed to have represented as much as

40 per cent of the Palestinian population. By 2009 mass emigration had slashed the number to less than 5 per cent. According to the *2010 CIA World Factbook*, in 2009 the Arab Christian population numbered 167,000 in the West Bank and 10,000 in Gaza, while it was 123,000 in Israel (about 10 per cent of the Arab Israeli population). Both the founder of the Popular Front for the Liberation of Palestine, George Habash, and Nayif Hawatmeh, the founder of its offshoot the DFLP, were Christians, as is prominent Palestinian activist and former Palestinian Authority minister Hanan Ashrawi. Today most Palestinian Christians (about three million, representing about 30 per cent of the total Palestinian population worldwide, which is estimated to be 10.1 million) live in the Diaspora. Reasons for this include the rise of Islamic radical movements in the Palestinian homeland.

Dr Hanna Iesa, Assistant Deputy Minister for Christian matters in the Palestinian Ministry of Awqaf, told the Arabic newspaper *Elaph* that the emigration of Christians from the Palestinian Territories, especially from Jerusalem, has recently become a warning sign. Quoting recent censors which put the number of those still leaving at around six hundred yearly, he said that the number of Christians in Jerusalem has come down from 50,000 to 10,000. Hanna added that about 125,000 Palestinian Christians from Bethlehem and Beth Jala have recently emigrated to the West. (*Elaph*, 13 April 2010)

Lebanon

Lebanon has the largest percentage of Christians of all the Middle Eastern nations. Lebanese Christians belong mostly to the Maronite Catholic Church, with sizable minorities of Greek Orthodox and Melkite Greek Catholics. There are also many Roman Catholics in the country, as a result of French rule, and most of them are of French descent. When modern Lebanon's constitution was drawn up in 1926, it specified a balance of power between the various religious groups. On the basis of the 1932 census, which stated that Christians made up 54 per cent of the population, parliament seats were divided according to a six-to-five Christian-Muslim ratio. Thus Lebanese Christians became the only Christians in the Middle East with a sizable political role in the country where the Lebanese president, half of the cabinet, half of the parliament are of the various Lebanese Christian sects. However, as there has been no official census in Lebanon since 1932, the number of Christians has been disputed for many years.

Since the Lebanese Civil War between 1975 and 1990, the country has experienced a large migration of Lebanese Christians, who have moved to North and South America, Europe and Australia. Today, according to recent statistics by the CIA Factbook, 59.7 per cent of the Lebanese population is Muslim, while 40 per cent (about 1,800,000) are Christians.

Egypt

The Coptic Christian population in Egypt is the largest Christian community in the Middle East. About 95 per cent of Egypt's Christians are members of the Coptic Orthodox Church of Alexandria. This is an Oriental Orthodox Church established in the first century AD by St Mark the evangelist. Today, Egyptian Christians are estimated to make up between 10 and 20 per cent of a population of over 80 million, though estimates vary.

32

The Copts in Modern Egypt

As the Copts had been treated badly by their Byzantine masters, they welcomed the arrival of the Muslim Arabs in 641, hoping for salvation. The political and religious conflict between the Copts and the rulers of Byzantium had started in the fifth century, when the Council of Chalcedon initiated the great schism on 451, which separated the Egyptian Church from Catholic Christendom. Coptic Christians were Monophysites who believed that after the incarnation Christ had but one nature with dual aspects. The council, however, declared that Christ had two natures and that he was equally human and equally divine. The Coptic Church refused to accept the council's decree and rejected the bishop sent to Egypt. Thenceforth, the Coptic Church was in schism from the Catholic Church as represented by the Byzantine Empire and the Byzantine Church.

For nearly two centuries, Monophysitism in Egypt became the symbol of national and religious resistance to Byzantium's political and religious authority, while the Egyptian Church was severely persecuted by Byzantium. Churches were closed, and Coptic Christians were killed, tortured, and exiled in an effort to force the Egyptian Church to accept Byzantine orthodoxy. The Coptic Church, however, continued to appoint its own patriarchs, refusing to accept those chosen by Constantinople and attempting to depose them. The break with Catholicism in the fifth century converted the Coptic Church into a national church with deeply rooted traditions that have remained unchanged to this day. By the seventh century, religious persecution and the growing pressure of taxation had engendered great hatred of the Byzantines, the result of which was the Egyptians' support to the conquering armies of Islam.

Muslim invasion

When Amr ibn al-'As arrived in Egypt, the Copts were suffering Byzantine oppression, which led Bishop Benyamin to escape and hide in the desert. When he knew of the Muslims' arrival, Benyamin cheered at the approaching end of Byzantine rule in Egypt. He asked the people of Egypt to help the coming Arabs, against the Byzantines. After the Byzantines' departure, Amr brought Bishop Benyamin and provided him with security. Benyamin went on to strengthen his Church and rebuild the monasteries and churches which had been destroyed before the Muslim invasion. He also sent an archbishop to Abyssinia, his final work being the establishment of a new church for St Makarios at the Matron Valley. (Ibn Abdul Hakam, *Futuhat Mir*, p. 58–9; Takikh ibn Al-Batriq, p. 21)

During the early days of Islamic rule, conversions of Copts to Islam were very rare, and the old system of taxation under Byzantium rule was maintained for the greater part of the first Islamic century. In return for a tribute of money and food for the occupying troops, the Egyptians were left to observe their religion and administrate their own affairs. After the Islamic takeover, the old Byzantine administration remained as it had been before, with some Byzantine officials, although others were replaced by Copts. During this early Islamic period, the Copts constituted a hereditary class experienced in financial and administrative matters. They were also given many positions in the administrative body of the state. (Qasim Abdo, *Ahl Adh-Dhimma*, p. 37)

However, the situation started to change under the Umayyad Dynasty (661–750). The increase in taxation led to some outbreaks of violence in 725, 739 and 750. Islam did not start to spread in Egypt before the eighth century, and neither did the Arabic language replace Coptic in official circles before the time of the Umayyad Caliph Abdul Malik bin Marawan around the end of the seventh century. Even after that date, Coptic remained in use together with Arabic until the Abbasid period.

The Abbasid caliphate, which started in Baghdad in 750, was marked by new taxations, and the Copts rebelled again in the fourth year of their rule. In 870 Ahmed Ibn Tulun, the ruler sent by the Abbasid caliph to govern Egypt, made himself independent of Baghdad and established his own ruling dynasty. The Tulunids (870–905) and the Ikhshdis which followed them (935–69) were tolerant towards the Christian communities and, except for Caliph al-Hakim (996–1021), who ordered the sacking of monasteries and churches and dismissed Copts from government offices, the Copts also enjoyed good times under the Fatimids (969–1171). Under the Fatimids, government offices were packed by Christians and Jews, especially in the first period, who occupied even the posts of ministers and heads of offices. Coptic employees spread through all administrative and financial offices, because of their skill in financial matters. They were more experienced in collecting tribute and tax. The doctors of the caliph's palace were chosen from among the Dhimmis because of their mastery in medical treatment and medicine. (*Ahl Adi-Dhimma fi Masr fi Al-'Asr Al-Fatimi Al-Awwal*, p. 27)

The arrival of the Crusaders in the Levant had negative consequences for Christians throughout the area. Syrian Christians fled to Egypt to take refuge, but in

> Egypt itself, the Crusaders did not distinguish between Muslims and the anti-Chalcedonian Christians; Copts were adjudged heretics. At the same time, Crusader victories led to severe retaliatory actions against the Copts, for Muslim rulers did not distinguish between the indigenous Christians and the invaders. When Egypt's first Ayyubid ruler, Salah al-Din (Saladin, 1171–93), came to power, he dismissed Copts from government offices. He obliged all Copts to wear distinctive dress and forbade them to ride horses. The great Cathedral of St Mark in Alexandria was destroyed on the pretext that the Crusaders might fortify it should they take the city. However, the Ayyubid sultans (1171–1250), were in general relatively tolerant of the Copts, so that in 1218 the Egyptian Christians joined forces with them to battle the Crusaders who had captured the north-eastern Delta town of Damietta. The Mamluks who followed the Ayyubid in ruling Egypt were slaves, brought mainly from the region of the Caspian

> and Black Seas and sold and trained in Egypt as soldiers. They assumed power in 1250 and ruled Egypt until 1517. The fortunes of the Copts declined steadily throughout this period, and by the time of the Ottoman invasion their situation was catastrophic. They were often dismissed from government offices. Humiliating rules and refutations were frequently enforced . . . On one day in 1321, fanatic Muslims sacked and burned over 60 of the main churches and monasteries throughout Egypt. The art of wall painting with its long tradition in Coptic monasteries and churches deteriorated remarkably and finally ceased during this era.
>
> [Gawdat Gabra, *Historical Dictionary of the Coptic Church*, Scarecrow Press, 2008, p. 5]

Coptic feasts

Although their country was ruled by Muslims, Egyptians were allowed to practise their old traditions without interference. Some Coptic feasts even became national occasions under the Islamic State, such as the Nile feast. Muslims took part in celebrating Coptic feasts and shared in the manifestation of courtesy, exchanging food, sweets and presents. The most famous of these feasts was the Feast of the Martyr, which took place yearly on the eighth of the Coptic month of Bashans. There was a common ancient belief that the volume of the Nile would not increase during the flood season unless the 'Martyr's finger' were thrown into the river. They used to keep the Martyr's finger, which belonged to one of the Coptic saints, in a coffin at a church in the area of Shobra. (Sobh Al-A'sha, *Al-Qakqashandi*, part 13, p. 263) The Martyr's feast was one of the best pleasure outings in Egypt, and the Christians travelled from villages all over the country to ride horses and play. In Cairo, ordinary people of different classes went out and raised their tents on the banks of the Nile and its islands, for fun. All singers, male and female, and entertainers went out to take part in this feast. Many people gathered, and so much money was spent that it was impossible to estimate. This gathering always took place in the Shobra area of Cairo.

However, this feast was finally stopped around 1302, in the time of Al-Malik An-Nasir Muhammad Qlawun (the Abbasside caliph) and Prince Run Ad-Din Baybars (the governor). Baybars ordered that the Martyr's finger should not be thrown into the Nile; neither should it be celebrated as a feast. He ordered the governor of Cairo to prevent people from gathering at Shobra as usual. He also sent letters to the governors in all parts of Egypt, to announce that no Christian should go out to celebrate the Martyr's feast. (Hosn Al-Muhadara, *As-Suyuty*, part 2, p. 299)

The Copts used also to celebrate the Nayrouz feast, which represented the new Coptic year at the beginning of the Coptic month of Toot. This was a Pharaonic feast. Nayrouz was celebrated in Egypt until as recently as the time of the Mamluks, four and half centuries ago. It was a national feast in Egypt and a public holiday, when markets and schools closed and people gathered in the streets of Cairo before joining the festival. At the head of their procession rode a man on a donkey; he would have a tall hat on his head, his face painted white, and he would wear a false beard and a yellow dress. The donkey rider held a notebook in his hand, surrounded by dates and green palms. This procession used to go around, marching through Cairo's streets, entering markets to collect money, while the public threw eggs and water at each other. People ate sweets during the feast; also *zalabia* (pancake) and *harisa* (mash), together with watermelon, peach and dates. (Qasim Abdo, *Ahl Adh-Dhimma*, Qasim Abdo, p. 155)

Muslims also took part in the Christian celebrations for Christmas on 7 January, when they cooked *'Asida*, a kind of porridge, to protect them from the winter cold. Maqrizi, the Egyptian historian who himself lived during the Mamluk era, witnessed Christmas celebrations where candles and coloured lanterns were hung in the market place. During Epiphany, some Muslims joined the Copts in dipping their children in water, in spite of its being cold, while on Covenant Thursday Christians offered their neighbours lentils, coloured eggs and fried fish. Women went out on this day to buy incense. (Ibid., pp. 155–6)

The Ottomans

Under Ottoman rule, which lasted for about three centuries, the vast majority of Egypt's inhabitants endured one of the most impoverished periods in their long history. However, the Christians were left to lead a relatively peaceful existence trying to preserve what remained of their ancestors' religious legacy. A significant factor that sustained the existence of the Copts under the Mamluk and Ottoman empires was their success in financial administration, coupled with a comparatively pacific disposition. (Gawdat Gabra, *Historical Dictionary of the Coptic Church*, p. 6)

Muhammad Ali

Modern Egypt was born with the arrival of the French expedition to Abukir (east of Alexandria) at the end of the eighteenth century, led by Napoleon Bonaparte. For, although the French army managed to occupy the country for three years (1798–1801), they did help the people of Egypt to get rid of their Mamluk oppressors. With the Mamluks out of power and the French occupation ended, Muhammad Ali, a young officer who had been second in command of an Albanian contingent sent by the Ottoman government to evacuate the French, stepped in to fill this vacuum. He established a local power base of village leaders, clerics, and wealthy merchants in Cairo. When the Egyptian leaders chose Muhammad Ali to be their ruler, he was recognised by the Ottomans in Istanbul as the sultan's *wali* or viceroy of Egypt.

After eighteen hundred years of being part of different foreign empires, Muhammad Ali rebuilt Egypt as a separate political entity. He decided to modernise the country with modern education, and re-shaped Egyptian agricultural economy. Ali began to conscript peasants from Upper Egypt, for the first time since the fall of Pharaonic Egypt, to be trained under a French officer, Colonel Sèves (Suleyman Pasha). Those troops were based on a regular draft pattern and organised along contemporary European schemes. The needs of the military fuelled different modernisation projects, such as state educational institutions, a teaching hospital, roads and canals, factories to turn out uniforms and munitions, and a ship-building foundry at Alexandria.

Eventually, in 1840, the main powers in Europe signed the London Convention, which granted Muhammad Ali hereditary rule over Egypt- although technically, the Ottoman Turks continued to rule Egypt until 1922. As a result of this separation from the Ottoman Empire, the Egyptians asserted a new sense of pride and a new Egyptian nationalism was born. Egypt's independent rule did not last for long, however; the British army would occupy the country in 1882. The outbreak of World War I brought Egypt formally into the British Empire as a Protectorate. Nevertheless, Egyptian nationalism continued to grow under British occupation, and a constitution was written which resulted in the establishment of parliamentary democracy. By the end of World War II, the Egyptian nation was ready to fight, not only to achieve its political independence, but also to regain its long lost memory and establish its national identity.

During the rule of Muhammad Ali and his dynasty (1805–1952), the Copts flourished. Their churches and monasteries were restored, and the *jizya* imposed was abolished in 1855 as the Copts became full citizens. Muhammad Ali and most of his descendants encouraged all Egyptians to build a modern Egypt, regardless of religious identity. However, during the first half of the twentieth century, the nationalistic movement against the British occupation of Egypt took Islamic banners, calling for the return of the Ottoman rule.

> In 1910, Egypt's prime minister, Butros Ghali, a Copt, was assassinated by a Muslim partisan of the Nationalist Party. This crime led to serious clashes between Copts and Muslims. National unity was achieved only by the revolution of 1919, which pitted both against the British occupation. The emblem of this uprising – a crescent enclosing a cross – reflected the bond between Muslims and Copts who were exiled with the revolution leader, Sa'd Zaghlul, and jailed for their part in the

> struggle for its independence. Undoubtedly, Sa'd Zaghlul succeeded in unifying Muslims and Copts in his Wad party. In 1923, Copts comprised nearly 44 per cent of its executive committee. The three decades following the revolution of 1919 represented a liberal period that was characterised by excellent relations between Muslims and Copts.
>
> The situation changed completely in the second half of the twentieth century, after the fall of Muhammd Ali's dynasty. Following the 1952 *coup d'état* by the Free Officers, the conditions of the Copts have been slowly deteriorating and their human rights are often violated. Under the regime of President Gamal Abd el-Nasser (1954–70), many wealthy Christian families lost their real estate and other property. His land reforms also weighed heavily on the Coptic patriarchate and on land-holding Coptic monasteries. Copts were dramatically under-represented in high government positions, in the army, and on the faculties of universities. A few 'token' Copts were nominated to sit in Parliament to demonstrate that they were represented in the political structure. But for practical purposes, Copts no longer played a role in politics . . . Muslim militants plundered and set fire to Coptic shops, especially jewellers and pharmacies at el-Minya and Assut [provinces], and attacked churches in villages throughout Upper Egypt. [Ibid., p. 6]

Nasser's mainstream policy was pan-Arab nationalism and socialism. The Copts were severely affected by Nasser's nationalisation policies because, although they represented about 20 per cent of the population, they were so economically prosperous that they held more than 50 per cent of the country's wealth.

In addition, Nasser's pan-Arab policies undermined the Copts' strong attachment to their Egyptian identity. Although in 2002, under the Mubarak government, Coptic Christmas (7 January) was recognised as an official holiday, many Copts continue to complain of being minimally represented in law enforcement, state security and public office, and of being discriminated against in the work force on the basis of their religion. Most Copts do not support independence or separation from other Egyptians. As a result, many Copts have left their country for Australia, North America or Europe. Since 1971, under Pope Shenouda III, many Coptic churches have been established in the US, Canada, Australia, Europe and Africa.

At the same time, since 1952, religious freedom in Egypt has been hampered to varying degrees by discriminatory and restrictive government policies. Copts have faced increasing marginalisation after the military coup and, until recently, Christians were required to obtain presidential approval even for minor repairs in churches. Although the law was eased in 2005 by handing down the authority of approval to the governors, Copts continue to face many obstacles and restrictions in building new churches.

> According to statistics compiled by the Centre for Human Rights, Muslim fundamentalists have committed 561 acts of violence against Copts since 1994. In the past twenty-five years, militants have slaughtered foreign tourists, and attacked churches in their insurgency against the Egyptian government under President Hosni Mubarak. Most Muslim politicians and intellectuals strongly condemn these criminal activities, which have contributed to the emigration of large numbers of Copts to the United States, Canada, and Australia since the 1960s. [Ibid., p. 7]

Conclusion

The claim of political Islamic groups that they represent true Islam has no foundation. Those who kill innocent people in the name of Allah, have no authority from the Qur'an or from the Prophet of Islam. Muhammad established Islam as a religion, faith and worship, and introduced the Qur'an as its holy book. He also united the Arabian tribes in a nation *(umma)*, which included some non-Islamic elements. It was Abu Bakr, the first caliph, who fought to create the Islamic state and forced the Arab tribes to pay *zakat*, which he regarded as a poll tax. It was Umar ibn al Khattab, the second caliph, who established the first Islamic state and created Sharia Law to organise his new government.

The main aim of political Islam is to overthrow the ruling government in different Muslim countries by force and create a new universal caliphate that would subdue all nations of the world, in order to establish what they believe to be the holy rule of God. This is a new belief, one that was not part of the Islam that was preached by Muhammad. There is no single mention, either in the Qur'an or in the Prophet's tradition, of an Islamic government. The modern Arabic word for 'to rule', '*hakama*', was not used in the Qur'an to indicate a ruling power in a political state, but to mean 'arbitration'. 'If thou judge, judge in equity between them . . . ' (5:42) and: 'They can have no (real) faith, until they make thee judge in all disputes between them, and find in their souls no resistance against thy decisions.' (4:65) On the other hand, the tribal chiefs were still ruling their tribes while Muhammad was alive, and they are referred to in the Qur'an as '*uli al-Amr minhum*', 'those with authority among them'. (4:83)

Political Islam is a new attempt to revive not Islam as a religion, but the Islamic caliphate which was dissolved by the Turks after World War II. Unless those who believe in Islam as being a faith and religion, who are the great majority of Muslims, can positively identify themselves away from the new wave of political Islam, confusion will go on, not only in the West, but also at home, as to what Muhammad really looked like.

There is no doubt that Muslim countries do have some political problems with the Christian West, but these can only be resolved by peaceful means. There is no need for violent confrontation. Now that political Islam has managed to give the world a wrong picture about our religion, it is time for us Muslims to feel proud of our own heritage and shout in anger and put an end to their claim to represent us. This is not our Islam.

Bibliography

Abdo, Qasim, *Ahl Adh-Dhimma fi Misr*, Ain for Social Studies and Researches, Cairo, 2003

Ali, Abdullah Yusuf, *The Meaning of the Glorious Quran*, Lahore, 1976

Ali, Jawad, *Tarikh al-Arab Qabl al-Islam*, 8 volumes, Baghdad, 1950–9

Ali, Salih Ahmed, *Mukhtarat fi Tarikh al-Arab: The Life of Muhammad and Islamic Preaching in Mecca*, Baghdad, 1955

Andare, Tor, *Muhammad*, translated from German by Theophil Menzel, Allen & Unwin, London, 1936

Baladhuri, Ahmad ibn Yahya, *Futuh al-Buldan*, Dar al-Andalus, translated by Philip Khuri Hitti, Columbia University, New York, 1916–1924

Bell, Richard, *The Quran*, translated with a critical re-arrangement of the Suras, 2 volumes, T. Clark: Edinburgh, 1937–9, 1953

Bell, Richard, *The Origin of Islam*, Frank Cass, London, 1968

Belyaev, E. A., *Arabs, Islam and the Arab Caliphate in the Middle Ages*, translated by Adolphe Gourevitch, Frederick A. Praeger, New York, 1969

Birkeland, Harris, *The Lord Guideth*, Studies on Primitive Islam, H. Aschehoug, Oslo, 1956

Bishop, Eric F. F., *The Qumran Scrolls and the Quran*, Hartford Seminary Foundation, 1958

Box, G. H. and Landsman, J. I. (eds), *The Apocalypse of Abraham, Society for Promoting Christian Knowledge*, Macmillan, New York, 1919

Busse, Heribert; Lewis, Bernard (eds), *Islam, Judaism and Christianity*, Princeton, 1998

Gabra, Gawda, *Historical Dictionary of the Coptic Church*, Scarecrow Press, 2008

Global Arabic Encyclopedia, Riyadh, Saudi Arabia, 1996

Glubb, Sir John, *A Short History of the Arab Peoples*, Hodder and Stoughton, London, 1969

Goldziher, Ignaz, *Muslim Studies*, 2 volumes, translated by Stern, S. M., Aldine Transaction, New Edition 2005

Guillaume, Alfred, *The Traditions of Islam*, Oxford, 1924

Guillaume, Alfred, *Life of Muhammad: A Translation of Ibn Isshaq's Sirat Rasul Allah*, Oxford University Press, New York, 1955

Guillaume, Alfred, *New Light on the Life of Muhammad*, Journal of Semitic Studies, 1960

Ibn Abd al-Hakam, *Kitab Futuh Mis*, English translation by Charles C. Torrey, New Haven, 1922

Harris, Christina Phelps, *Nationalism and Revolution in Egypt*, Mouton, The Hague, London and Paris, 1964

Holt, P. M., Lambton, Ann K. S. and Lewis, Bernard, (eds), *The Cambridge History of Islam*, vol. 1, Cambridge University Press, 1970

Huntington, Samuel P., *The Clash of Civilizations and the Remaking of World Order*, Simon & Schuster, New York, 1996

Jomier, Jacque, *The Bible and the Quran*, Ignatius Press, 2002

Juynboll, G. H. A., *The Authenticity of the Traditional Literature, Discussions in Modern Egypt*, Leiden, 1969

Katsh, Abraham I., *Judaism in Islam*, New York University Press, 1954

Khan, Muhammad M. (tra), *Sahih al-Bukhari*, Dar-us-Salam, 1997

Levi della Vida, Giogrgio, *Sira*, Encyclopaedia of Islam, E. J. Brill, Leiden, `9`3–`936

Lewis, Bernard, *Islam and the West*, Oxford University Press, New York and Oxford, 1993

Lewis, Bernard, *The Crisis of Islam*, Modern Library, 2003

Mansfield, Peter, *The Arabs*, Allen Lane, London, 1976

Margolioth, David Samuel, *The Relations between Arabs and Israelites prior to the Rise of Islam*, British Academy, London, 1924

Ibn al-Muqaffa, Sawirus, *History of the Patriarchs of the Coptic Church of Alexandria*, Paris: Firmin, 1907–1915

Murphy, Caryle, *Passion for Islam: Shaping the Modern Middle East: the Egyptian Experience*, Simon and Schuster, New York, 2002

Pearson, Birger A., and Goehring, James E. (eds), *The Roots of Egyptian Christianity*, Fortress Press, Philadelphia, 1986

Pearson, Birger A., *Gnosticism, Judaism, and Egyptian Christianity*, Fortress Press, 1990

Rabin, Chaim, *Qumran Studies*, Oxford University Press, 1957

Rodinson, Maxime, *Mahomet*, translated from the French by Ann Carter, Allen Lane, London, 1971

Ibn Saad, *At-Tabaqat al-Kubra*, edited by al-Abdeh Mohammad, Glasgow University, 2003

Ibn Saad, Haq, S. M. (trans.), *Al-Tabaqat*, Kitab Bhavan, 1990

Sahas, Daniel J., *John of Damascus on Islam*, Leiden: E. J. Brill, 1972

Al-Suyuty, *Jalal al-Den*, Husn al-Muhadara, Cairo, 1324

Swartz, Merlin L. (trans. and ed.), *Studies on Islam*, Oxford, 1981

Torrey, Charles C., *The Jewish Foundation of Islam*, Jewish Institute of Religion Press, New York, 1933

Walsh, P. G. (tr), *The Poems of St Paulinus of Nola*, Newman Press, New York, 1975

Watt, W. Montgomery, and McDonald, M. V. (eds and trs), *The History of al-Tabari: Muhammad at Mecca*, State University of New York Press, Albany, 1988

Young, F. M., *Judaism and Islam*, Madras, 1898

Index

Aamina (mother of Muhammad) 13–15, 53
Aaron 49, 66–7
al-Abbas (uncle of Muhammad) 54–5, 91, 129
Abbasid Dynasty 128–31, 144, 181–2
Abd al-Muttalib 12, 13, 15, 17, 53, 71
Abd al-Wahhab, Muhammad 137
Abdullah ibn Abd al-Muttalib 13–14
bin Abd Manaf, Hashim 11, 14, 19, 71
ibn Abi Rabi'a, Abdullah 38–9
Abraham 8, 9, 26, 48, 49, 50, 107, 120
Abu Ayyub bin Zaid 59
Abu Bakr, Caliph
  before Caliphate 22, 32, 35, 58–9, 95–6
  as Caliph 114–17, 119–20, 124, 189
Abu Haritha ibn Alqama 78–9
Abu Jahl 34, 41, 43, 47, 58
Abu Lahab 46
Abu Qir 135, 136
Abu Sufyan 90, 91
Abu Talib (uncle of Muhammad)
  birth of 13
  death of 44–5
  as head of Hashemites 16, 43
  and prophecy of Buhayra 17–18
  protects Muhammad 33–4, 36, 42, 105–6
bin Abu Talib, Jafar 39
Abu Umama 53, 54, 69
Abyssinia (Ethiopia) 36–7, 38–9
Acts of Mark 150, 151
Adam 48, 50, 108, 120
ibn Adi, Mut'im 47
Aedesius 37
bin Affan, Caliph Uthman 32, 37–8, 120, 164
Al-Ahram Weekly (newspaper) 4, 5
Ajnadayn (battle) 125
Alexandria 125, 135, 145–8, 149–52, 161–3
ibn al-'As, Amr 38–9, 125, 144, 148, 158–63
Al-Jazeera (television station) 3
Al-Qa'ida 1, 3, 5, 101–2, 173
Ali, Caliph (son of Abu Talib) 23, 28, 59, 126–7
Ali, Muhammad 136, 137–8, 185–7
Alshehri, Waleed 1
bin Amr Al-Aamiri, Hisham 43
Ananias, Bishop 150–1
Andrae, Tor 107
Ansar 53–5, 58, 68–71, 73, 77, 95, 114–16
Arab League 4, 171

Arab nationalism 165–7, 171–2
El Arish 158–9
Asad (clan) 19
bin Asad, Amr 21
Assembly of the Synod 175–6
Ataturk, Mustafa Kemal 140, 164
Athanasius, Pope 37
Atlantic Monthly (magazine) 5
Atta, Mohammad 1, 2, 3
al-Aw (tribe) 55, 56–7, 61, 65–6, 68
ibn al-Awan, Zubair 160, 161
Ayesha 22, 59–60, 94–5, 114, 126

Babilyon (fortress) 125, 158, 159–61
Badr (battle) 63, 64
Baghdad 129, 130–1
el-Banna, Hassan 168, 169, 170
Banu Bakr (tribe) 10, 90–1
Banu Kaynuqa (tribe) 56–7, 63–4, 70–1
Banu Nadir (tribe) 56–7, 63, 64–5, 70–1, 90
Banu an-Najjar (tribe) 11–13, 52–3, 63, 69, 71
Banu Qurayza (tribe) 56, 63, 65–6, 70–1
al-Bara 55
Benedict XVI, Pope 175–6
Benyamin, Bishop 148, 162–3, 181
Bilal 35
Bin Laden, Osama 1–4, 101–2, 173–4
Boukolou 151
Buhayra 17–18, 20
Buraq (winged horse) 48
Byzantium Empire 123–4, 125, 147, 180–1

Church of the Holy Sepulchre 51, 132
Constantine, Emperor 147, 153, 155
Constantinople 127, 129, 131, 134, 140
Constitution of Medina 60–2
Coptic Orthodox Church 37, 149, 179
Copts 145, 163, 171, 175, 179
  persecution of 146–8, 180–3, 187–8
Cordoba 128, 133, 139
Crusades 132–3, 182
Cyril II, Pope 37
Cyrus (governor of Egypt) 160–1

Damascus 29, 125, 127, 166–7, 168
David 82–3
Dead Sea Scrolls 71, 72, 75
Dhimmis 127, 142–4, 171
Dhu-Nuwas, King of Yemen 77–8

Egypt
  Arab conquest of 125, 144, 158–63, 181–4
  Byzantine occupation of 147–8
  Copts in *see* Copts
  French occupation of 135–6
  modernisation of 138
  monasticism in 153–7
  Ottoman occupation of 185–6
  Roman occupation of 145–7
  tax system of 144, 163, 181–2
Egyptian Coptic Church 37, 149
Ella Amida, King of Abyssinia 37
Essenes of Qumran (sect) 71–6
Ethiopian Orthodox Church 37
Eusebius, Bishop 149

Ezana, King of Abyssinia 37

Faysal, Prince 166–7
Five Pillars of Islam 104
Frumentius 37

Gabriel (angel)
  and Mary 81–2, 85–6
  and Muhammad 26–8, 29–30, 48–50, 119
Geiger, Abraham 108–9
Genghis Khan 130
Ghali, Butros 186
El-Ghazali Harb, Osama 4–5
Global Arabic Encyclopedia 6

Hadith 105, 121
Hagar 8, 9, 97
Hajj (pilgrimage) 6, 8, 10, 11, 32, 94, 104
Halima (nursemaid of Muhammad) 15
Hamza (*Lion of God*) 21, 41, 52
Hanifs 24–5, 73
Hanjour, Hani 1
bin al-Harith, Auf 53
Hashemites 11, 14, 19, 33, 43–4, 46, 47
Hashim bin Abd Manaf 11, 14, 19, 71
Heraclius, Emperor 90, 97, 125, 158, 160–2
Hijaz 56, 108, 137, 166, 167–8
Hijra 58, 63
Hira (cave) 24, 25, 26, 73
bin Hizam, Hakim 43
House of Wisdom 130
Hubal 10
Hudaybiya 90–1
Hunayn (battle) 93
Huntington, Samuel P. 5
Husayn (son of Caliph Ali) 126, 127
Hussein, Saddam 177
Hussein, Sharif 165–7, 168

Ibn Abbas 19–20, 22–3
Ibn Hisham 13, 15, 17, 27, 36, 86, 105–6
Ibn Ishaq 13, 15, 17, 30, 42, 60
Ibn Kathir 86, 141
Ibn Saud 167–8
Iraq 124, 126–7, 177
Isaiah 88
Ishmael 8, 9, 97
Israel 4–5, 170, 176–8
Italy 127, 130

Jabal An-Nur (Mountain of Light) 24, 25
ibn Jarir al-Tabari, Muhammad 12, 13
al-Jarrah, Ziyad 1
al-Jazeera (television station) 3
Jerusalem 47–8, 50–1, 73, 125, 132, 158
Jesus Christ
  birth of 26, 81–2
  judgement of 110–11
  as Messenger of God 87–8, 98
  as Messiah 70, 72, 84–5
  met by Muhammad 48
  resurrection of 83–4, 111
  in the Qur'an 39–40, 85–8
jihad 3, 5, 101–2, 172–4
jizya 143–4, 160–1, 163, 171, 186
John of Damascus 97–9
John the Baptist 48, 83

Jordan 140, 176–7
Joseph 48, 81
Josephus 72, 152
Jyllands-Posten (newspaper) 102
Kaaba (sanctuary) 9, 10, 12, 15, 28, 92
Kadisiyya (battle) 124
Khadija (wife of Muhammad)
  death of 44, 59
  marries Muhammad 19–23
  and Muhammad's prophethood 27–8, 29
  smuggles water to Hashemites 43–4
  supports Muhammad 22, 28–30, 33, 44
Khalid ibn Walid 116, 123–4, 125, 160
ibn Al-Khattab, Umar *see* Umar, Caliph
al-Khazraj (tribe) 55, 56–7, 68
Khomeini, Ayatollah 101, 102
bin Kilab, Qusai 10, 58
Khuzaa (tribe) 10
Kufa 126

bin Laden, Osama 1–4, 101–2, 173–4
al-Lat 13, 18, 28
League of Nations 167
Lebanon 178–9
Levant 10–11, 14, 17, 20, 125
Lewis, Bernard 5, 164–5
Lote Tree 49

Mary 26, 39–40, 81–3, 85–6, 87, 98
Maseeh, Abdul 78, 79
al-Masjid al-Aqsa ('Distant Mosque') 47–8, 50–1
al-Masjid al Haram ('Sacred Mosque') 47
Maysara 20
Mecca
  captured by Muhammad 91–2
  captured by Wahhabis 137, 167
  famine in 23
  holy status of 8–9, 168
  Muhammad's war with 3–4, 78
  Muslims persecuted in 35, 36, 38
  pilgrimage to 6, 8, 10, 11, 32, 94, 104
Medina (Yathrib)
  captured by Wahhabis 137
  Jews expelled from 63–6, 68
  mosque built 59, 60, 71
  Muslim community established 54, 60–2
  origins of 55–7
  trade routes 8, 11
Milan Declaration (313AD) 147
Moses 26, 27, 48, 49, 54, 66–7, 72, 98
Mount of Olives 83
Mountain of Light (Jabal An-Nur) 24, 25
Moussa, Amr 4
Mu'awiya 126, 127
Mubarak, President Hosni 188
Muhammad, Prophet
  adopts Ali (son of Abu Talib) 23
  becomes leader of Banu an-Najjar 69
  begins preaching 31
  birth of 8, 14, 15
  builds mosque in Medina 59, 71
  buries wife (Khadija) 44
  business experience of 20

confirmed as a prophet 28
and Constitution of Medina 60–2
control of Arabia 78, 80, 89, 93, 112–14
death of 95–6, 114
destroys idols at Kaaba 92
Farewell Sermon of 94
as founder of Islam 7, 8
and Gabriel 26–7, 28, 29–30, 73, 119
and Hanifs 24–5
inspiration of 107–10
and Jews of Medina 63–6, 69–70, 75
journeys to Heaven 47–50
and King Negus 40
marries Ayesha 59–60
marries Khadija 20–2
meditation of 23–4, 73
meets Abraham, Moses and Jesus 48
as Messenger of Allah 6, 31, 39–40, 73
migrates to Medina 54–5, 58–9
and Najran Christians 78–80
orders followers to Abyssinia 36, 38
persecuted by Meccans 32–6, 45
physical appearance of 21–2
plot to kill 58–9
and prophecy of Buhayra 17–18
and Quraysh tribe 38, 42, 90
relationship with Khadija 22–3
sent to live with uncle (Abu Talib) 15–16
supported by Banu an-Najjar 52–3
travels to Ta'if 46
and use of violence 105–6
and wars with Mecca 4, 78, 89, 91–2
and Waraqa bin Nawfal 27–8
Western views of 97–102
wives of 59–60
Muir, William 100
Muslim Brotherhood Movement 168, 169–74

Naif Ibn Abdul Aziz, Prince 174
Najaf 127
Najd 137, 167, 168
Najjar *see* Banu an-Najjar (tribe)
Najran Christians 77–80
Napoleon Bonaparte 135–6, 184
Nasser, President Gamal Abdel 170, 171–2, 187
Nawfal (uncle of Abd al-Muttalib) 12–13
bin Nawfal, Waraqa 14, 19, 25, 27–8
Nayrouz feast 184
Negus, King of Abyssinia 39–40
Nelson, Lord 136
Nestor 20
Nicephorus I, King 129
Nufaysa (friend of Khadija) 21

Ottoman Empire 134–7, 138–40, 165–7, 185–6

Palestine 56, 72, 132, 140, 157, 171, 176–8
pan-Arabism 171–2, 187
Pelusium 159
Persian Empire 123–4

Pliny the Elder 72

al-Qa'ida 1, 3, 5, 101–2, 173
Qumran sect (Essenes) 71–6
Qur'an
 and the Bible 107, 108, 120, 141–2
 composition of 121
 final verse of 94, 103
 and five pillars 104
 and Gabriel 26
 and Hanifs 24
 history of 119–22
 and Jesus 81–2, 85–8
 and *jihad* 173
 and light and darkness 74
 and Muhammad's war with Mecca 3–4
 and nature of Islam 6, 189
Quraysh (tribe)
 boycott Hashemites 43–4
 defeated at Badr 63
 and Hanifs 25
 links with Najjar tribe 11
 members convert to Islam 41–2
 and Muhammad 31, 33–4, 42, 90, 105–6
 origins of 8, 9, 10
 persecute Muslims 35, 36, 38
Qusai bin Kilab, 10, 58
Qutb, Muhammad 173–4
Qutb, Sayyid 172–3

Rabin, Chaim 71–2, 74–5
Ramadan 6, 24, 32, 104
al-Rashid, Caliph Harun 129, 130
al-Rashid, Caliph al-Mamun 130, 144
Rustem 124

Sa'ad (tribe) 15
Saladin 132–3, 182
Salma (wife of Hashim) 11–12, 14, 19, 53, 71
Sarah (wife of Abraham) 8, 9, 97
Saud (house of) 137, 167
Savary, Claude ƒtienne 101
September 11 attacks 1–5, 101–2
Serapis (Egyptian cult) 147, 151, 152, 155
Shari'a Law 6, 118, 142, 143, 169–70, 189
Shi'ite Muslims 105, 126–7
Sicily 127, 130
Siffeen (battle) 126
Spain 99, 128–9, 133
St Anthony 154–5, 157
St Athanasius 154, 157
St Jerome 155, 156
St Mark 149–52, 179, 182
St Pachomius 155–6
St Paul 29
St Paulinus 152
Sufism 101, 137
Sunnah (Sunna) 103, 104–5, 121
Sunni Muslims 105, 126–7
Sura of Kahf (The Cave) 36
Sura of Maryam (Mary) 39
Sura of Najm (The Star) 49
Sykes-Picot Agreement (1916) 140
Syria 124–6, 128–9, 136, 138, 140, 176–7

Ta'if 46, 47, 93
tawaf ritual 92
Temple Mount 51
Temple of Jupiter 51
Terah 50
bin Thabit, Hassan 15

The Apocalypse of Abraham (book) 50
The Crisis of Islam (book) 5
The Heresy of the Ishmaelites (book) 97–8
The History of al-Tabari (book) 13
The Life of Mahomet (book) 100
Time (magazine) 101
Turkey 140, 164–5

ibn Ubadah, Sa'd 114, 115
ibn Udas an-Najjari, Abu Sad 12–13
Umar ibn Al-Khattab, Caliph
  assassination of 126
  becomes Caliph 124
  captures Jerusalem 51, 125, 158
  converts to Islam 41–2
  and death of Muhammad 95
  establishes government 117–18, 169, 189
  expands Islamic Empire 124–5, 158, 162
  and succession of Muhammad 114–15
  supports Muhammad 52
Uhud (battle) 64
Umayyad Dynasty 126–7, 128–9, 144, 181
Umm Ayman 14, 15
Umm Habiba 90, 91
United Arab Republic 172
Uthman bin Affan, Caliph 32, 37–8, 120, 164
al-Uzza 18, 28

Voltaire 100

Wahhabism 137, 167, 168, 174
al Walid, Caliph 51
al-Waqidi 65
Waraqa bin Nawfal 14, 19, 25, 27–8
'Wars of Apostasy' 116
Wellhausen, Julius 24, 109–10
ibn Walid, Khalid 116, 123–4, 125, 160
World Trade Centre 1, 2

Yamama (battle) 119
Yarmouk (battle) 160
Yathrib *see* Medina
Yemen 77–8, 168

Zaghlul, Sa'd 186–7
Zakat 6, 32, 93, 104, 113–14, 116–17, 189
bint Zama, Sawda 59–60
Zamzam Well 9, 12
el-Zawaheri, Ayman 102
Zayd 31, 32
bin Zurara, As'ad 53, 54